WEEKEND WOOD PROJECTS FOR

TOYMAKERS

JEFF BURKE □ FIONA NEVILE □ RON FULLER □ DIK GARROOD

Sterling Publishing Co., Inc.   New York

CONTENTS

House Editor: **Donna Wood**
Technical Editor: **Aidan Walker**
Art Editor: **Gordon Robertson**
Photographer: **Peter Reilly**
Illustrator: **John Hutchinson**
Production: **Richard Churchill**

Published by Sterling, Publishing Co., Inc., Two Park Avenue, New York, N.Y. 10016

© Marshall Cavendish Limited 1987

ISBN 0–8069–6494–4 (paperback)
0–8069–6602–5 (hardback)

Typeset in 10/11pt Melior by J & L Composition, Filey, North Yorkshire
Printed and bound in Italy by L.E.G.O.S.p.a Vicenza

Provided you follow the instructions exactly the toys in this book should be as safe and strong as those you will find in the shops. If in any doubt as to their safety ask an experienced woodworker to check over the finished product before you put it into use. The Publishers and the individual toymakers cannot accept responsibility for any damage, loss or injury arising from the use or misuse of any of the toys in this book.

TOOLS & MATERIALS
UK/US EQUIVALENTS

UK	US
Bevel gauge	Bevel set
Craft knife	Stanley knife
Cramp(s)	Clamp(s)
Hardboard	Masonite
Panel pin	Finishing nail
Spanner	Wrench
Try & mitre square	Combination square

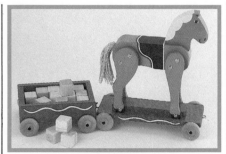

INTRODUCTION

Jeff Burke's toys are the epitome of well-made, simple craftsmanship. Jeff's Watt Knot Steam Company produces sturdy wooden trains and wheeled vehicles in a natural finish that brings out the beauty of the timber. Jeff has been a Guild member for many years.

Dik Garrood was an art teacher before he began making toys. In 1975 he started work for a toymaking company, developing the skills he now uses to such good effect in his own range of toys. He started his own business in 1983, and has already earned a fine reputation.

After leaving university, **Fiona Nevile** started her own toymaking business with her sister Sara. Apart from making her own range of brightly painted wooden toys which she sells from her stall at Covent Garden craft market, Fiona works as a freelance designer.

Ron Fuller taught at an art school before he became a full-time toymaker nearly twenty years ago. He produces his imaginative range of toys and automata from his workshop in Suffolk, and his willingness to give help and advice to other toymakers has earned him much respect in the trade.

All four of these contemporary craftspeople make a living out of toymaking, creating thriving businesses out of their natural talents and hobbies.

The toys they have designed for this book will give immense pleasure to any child, as well as encouraging creativity by developing the natural capacity for fantasy and imagination that all children possess. Manipulation and co-ordination skills will be encouraged by toys like the spinning top game. Numeracy and social skills will come from playing with the clock and the scales, and the mobile, when placed over a baby's cot, will stimulate and amuse for hours, as well as helping with early focussing and eye movement.

Don't be put off by the technicalities of working with wood. The twenty projects in this book have clear instructions and exploded diagrams as well as colour photographs to highlight any tricky stage in the making. If you have not done any woodwork before you could start with a simple toy to build up your confidence before you move on to a more ambitious project like, for instance, the doll's house.

Every effort has been made to ensure that the instructions for making these toys are as clear as possible. However, here are a few simple pointers that will help make every project that much easier.

READ IT!

 1 Read the instructions right through before you start, and study all the diagrams. Don't rush into anything; in many cases there are steps whose success depends on the step before being done correctly, so make sure you follow the sequence.

TIMBER

 2 The materials lists are designed for you to know the exact size you should cut the components, but they do show up an abiding problem of specifying timber sizes when it is bought PAR, or 'planed all round'. Timber comes in 'nominal' widths and thicknesses which are almost always significantly more than their actual sizes, because they are categorized before they are put through the planing machine.

This is why, although the materials list might say you should use 25x15mm/1x⅝in wood, the drawings will show dimensions for notches and joints that assume the actual size will be 22x12mm/⅞x½in. Measure your timber carefully when you bring it home, look at the drawings and dimensions carefully and work out whether you need to revise any dimensions.

3 Having worked out from the materials lists everything you need of each size, add it all up and add *at least 10%*. This is the minimum wastage allowance – you would be advised to add 25%. Also bear in mind that timber is sold in units based on feet, even though in the UK now you order in metres. But you cannot buy 2m of timber; you have to buy 2.1m (equivalent to 7ft) or 1.8m (equivalent to 6ft). This is important to understand if you use a timber yard, because they will not be interested in selling three pieces of wood 78mm/3⅛in long, two pieces 406mm/16in long, and so on. Smaller hardware and DIY stores will cut sizes for you, but rarely accurately, and it is much more expensive – and usually lower-quality.

When looking over timber check the weight – the drier pieces are lighter, and on the whole the drier the better. Get the straightest pieces you can find, then look carefully over the lengths, check the faces and edges for splits, knots, curly grain, and 'shakes', which are splits you can see in the endgrain. These may look slight when you buy the wood, but when it dries out at home, they can suddenly (overnight) appear as alarming cracks. Sheet materials come in 2440x1220mm/8x4ft sizes; if you don't need all that, you will probably have to use a smaller shop, which will give you smaller sizes at a proportionately higher price. Again, don't trust them to cut accurately square – buy oversize and trim it yourself. Phone before you go if you're buying softwood to ask them if they have first quality, sometimes known as 'unsorted'. 'Joinery' timber might sound good, but it is actually the fourth or fifth grade.

MARKING

4 The main components in each project are marked with letters. Always identify pieces as soon as you cut them with a pencil mark; if you have pairs or sets that go together, make sure you have marked the matching ends and sides, insides, bottoms, tops, or whatever you need to know to know exactly how it fits. Remember to sand the marks off before assembly.

MEASURING

5 Don't get confused with imperial and metric measuring systems – never mix them. Drill sizes and timber widths and thicknesses are *equivalents*, not exact translations; stick to one system and you can't go wrong. If you're metric, keep to millimetres.

TOOLS

6 The tools lists show everything you need for each job, but there is a basic kit which you need for every project, and there are other basic requirements. The first of these is a good work surface, preferably a bench with a vice. You can make a decent one in the garage, but buy the best vice you can afford and fit it so the top of the jaws is flush with the top of the bench. Portable folding workbenches are excellent, but often not big enough; if you take a large piece of thick ply or blockboard (at least 18mm/¾in) and fix a long batten down the centre, you can clamp that in the jaws of the portable bench to make a larger surface when you need it. The main tools you will always need are a pencil, try square, two sorts of rules – a 300mm/12in metal one and a flexible spring loaded one (at least 1800mm/6ft), a hammer, some chisels, a small plane like a block plane, an electric jigsaw, a coping or fretsaw, an electric drill and some good quality bits, pliers, pincers, a bradawl, a longer panel or crosscut saw, and some G-cramps.

FINISHING

7 Painting, varnishing and gluing present no problems if you remember a few basic rules; 'ordinary' white wood glue is known as PVA, or polyvinyl acetate, which is fine for most jobs; but (a) it isn't waterproof, and (b) it won't stick something that has been painted. You must either keep everything apart to paint it and mask off the gluing areas before you stick it all together, or you can use epoxy resin glue, which will stick painted parts. Paints and varnishes should always be non-toxic; modeller's enamels are good and hard-wearing, but need a long time to dry and a good smooth base, while poster or acrylic paints are much easier to use, but don't wear well.

PUBLISHER'S NOTE

Throughout this book American and British sets of measurements have been given for all projects. Standard American measurements for toy materials can be found under the heading Imperial.

BUNNY-GO-ROUND

The value of a mobile for a child in its cot is unlimited – it will help the development of early eye focussing and capture a baby's interest, providing valuable stimulation to certain parts of the brain. The fun children get from these visual toys doesn't stop when they become toddlers, and a simple but strongly coloured mobile like this will be a suitable decoration for the bedroom or playroom for years to come.

You can trace the rabbit shapes from the full-size drawing off the page; use tracing paper, then lay that down on carbon paper over card to make templates – ideal if you are making several things the same shape.

The templates may even come in useful later on, perhaps when the children themselves want to make decorations. Remember to trace the patterns of the bows round the rabbits' necks and the inner ears when you have the tracing paper taped down over your gridded drawing.

The rabbits in this design are all hanging at the same height, but there is no reason why you should not give them different lengths of string. You must make sure the mobile is balanced when you do this, however – it will mean a fair amount of experiment and re-tying of the kite string. The beads with holes in are a useful and decorative way of tying off the string, but a substantial knot will do if you cannot get the beads. The mobile also takes apart and packs flat – good for holidays!

1 Trace out the shapes of the rabbits on the card, and mark up the shapes of the hangers. Measure the maximum amount of ply you will need for each piece; then cut the ply up into blanks – an electric jigsaw is best for this if you have one. The grain should run along the long dimensions. Remember to transfer the ear and bow patterns on to tracing paper – you will need them later for painting.

2 Cut the hanger blanks exactly to a simple oblong size, then mark out the half-depth slots exactly in the middle of each. Be sure to measure the exact thickness of the ply for a good fit.

Cut them out with a tenon saw – you can drill a hole at the blind end of the slot to help you chop it out with a chisel. Trim and adjust the slots until the pieces fit into each other with top and bottom edges flush.

Mark out the curve on one piece, and clamp them together, remembering that the slots are in the top of one and the bottom of the other! Cut both pieces at once, held together with the clamp or in the vice. You can then go on to trim and sand the curves like this as well.

3 Transfer the four rabbit shapes on to the four blanks, and cut them all out. The coping saw is best for this, because you need control over the tight corners. A vice is best for holding the

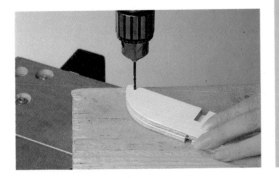

MATERIALS

Birch faced best plywood		Metric	Imperial
		400mm×300mm×12mm	15¼in×12in×½in
Small beads	6	6mm dia	¼in dia.
Braided nylon kite thread or fishing line		2m	7ft
Non-toxic acrylic or modelling enamel paints			
Non-toxic polyurethane varnish			

TOOLS

Pencil, tracing paper, sheets of paper, carbon, card	G-cramps
Steel rule, flexible rule	chisels 12mm/½in, 6mm/¼in
Try-square	Hand or electric drill
Coping saw or electric jigsaw	Drill bit 3mm/⅛in
Tenon saw	Medium and fine glasspaper
Small block plane or Surform shaper plane	Sanding block
	25mm/1in paintbrush
	Fine artist's brush

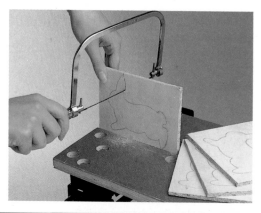

pieces during this operation, but you can manage with a work surface and a G-cramp – you will have to move the wood round and re-clamp every so often.

4 Drill the hanging holes in the backs of the rabbits and the tips of the hangers with the 3mm/⅛in bit. The holes in the hangers must be exactly the same distance from the ends.

Mark them out carefully on one piece, then clamp the other so it matches exactly, and drill through both at once while they are clamped tightly together.

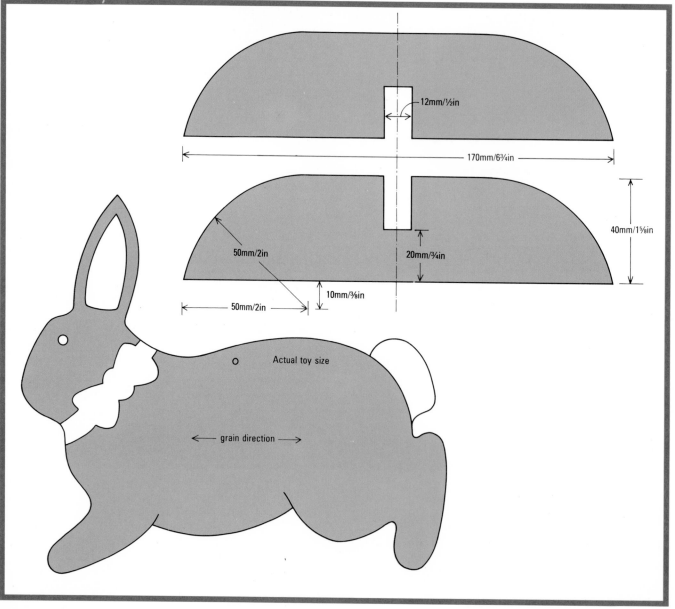

12mm/½in

170mm/6¾in

40mm/1⅝in

50mm/2in

20mm/¾in

10mm/⅜in

50mm/2in

Actual toy size

← grain direction →

5 Slot the hangers together and lay them flat on the work surface; you have to drill a vertical hole through both their centres – where they meet – but it must be vertical! Get help to 'sight' your drill in one direction while you concentrate on the other. If you have a drill stand, this is easy.

6 Sand all the components with medium and fine glasspaper, and paint them the base colours as in the photo. When they are dry, mark out the ear and bow patterns with the tracing paper or card templates you have made, and paint them in with the small artist's brush. Practise if you aren't confident, using a piece of scrap. Don't forget the blue eye-dots, or you will have blind rabbits.

When all the paint is dry, varnish the components.

7 Braided nylon string will need to be sealed with a match once you have cut it; cut four lengths of thread or line for the rabbits and one long one for the hanger.

Tie the rabbits up, then thread the line through the hanger holes and a bead, and tie a knot the other side of the bead. Adjust lengths for balance at the bead end.

Double the hanger length and knot it at one end, then slip a bead on and thread it through from under the hanger.

Slip a bead over the top, and knot the line on top of that with a knot you can undo easily so the mobile will take apart and pack flat.

HINT

If you cannot get any help drilling vertical holes, set the work up with two set-squares standing upright at 90° to each other, the blades towards the work, standing on the stocks. This gives you two vertical references, side to side and front to back.

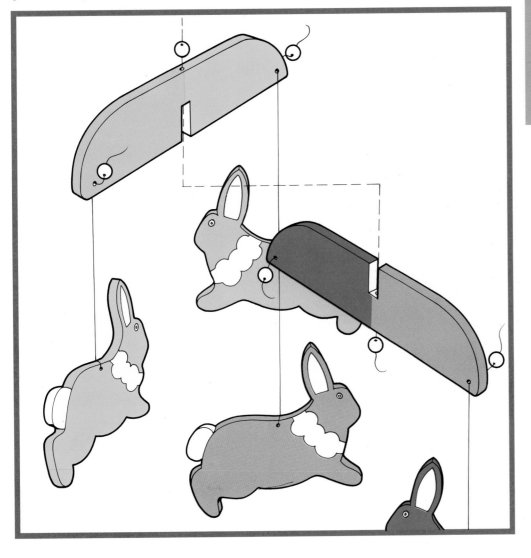

GO-KART, GO!

The classic go-kart needs no introduction for parents who have led a speed-crazed childhood! Slightly more sophisticated than the 'plank with wheels' originals, this design can be modified to suit any child; with the added comfort of a cushion or some padding to the seat back, or a foot rest nearer the seat to cater for smaller children. Learning to steer this craft will help co-ordination skills to develop. The go-kart also has the added safety speciality of a screw-hook and eye fixing for a broomstick or a piece of dowel which will act as a pusher and, more importantly, a safety restraint.

Even with this safety element in mind, however, it should be strongly emphasized that this is not really a toy, and that it should never be used in areas where there is even the slightest hint of danger, adult supervision or not.

Despite its stylish appearance, the kart could hardly be simpler to make. The main point to watch is the axles, which should be good quality and very firmly fixed. You should be able to get them from a pram and buggy supplier who also does repairs, along with the spring washer/dome hub-caps to hold the wheels on. The wheels themselves should come from the same source, although many good hardware stores will stock plastic wheels. Search for the wheels first, then work out what axles they need, and the size of the fixing clips. You can use the clips that hold surface bolts to a door, pipe clips from a plumber's merchant, or other fittings you might find in a hardware store or car accessory shop. Whatever you use, it's important that the axle fits neatly and that the clips are very strongly fixed.

MATERIALS

		Metric	Imperial
Birch faced best ply		850mm×480mm×12mm	33½in×19in×½in
Softwood (pine)			
Steering bar	1	360 × 75 ×25	14¼ × 3 ×1
Back axle mount	1	330 × 50 ×25	13 × 2 ×1
Wheels (plastic)	2	140 dia.	5½ dia.
	2	100 dia.	4 dia.
Steel axles	2	450	18
Washers	10	to fit axles	
Spring cap hubs	4	to fit axles	
Axle clips	7	to fit axles	
Screws			
Japanned r/head	14	no. 8 × 25	no. 8 × 1
Bright zinc csk	8	no. 8 × 25	no. 8 × 1
	6	no. 8 × 32	no. 8 × 1¼
Bolt	1	50mm (10mm dia.)	2in (⅜in dia.)
Nuts	2	to fit bolt; or 'Nyloc', one self-locking	
Washers	4	to fit bolt	
Hook	1	19mm (¾in) internal dia.	
Eye	1	to fit hook	
Dowel or broom stick		900mm (32mm dia.)	36in (1¼in dia.)
Nylon rope		1000mm (39in)	
Glasspaper, medium and fine			
Paint; primer, undercoat and non-toxic gloss, waterproof wood filler			

TOOLS

Pencil, paper
Try square
Steel rule, flexible rule
Electric jigsaw or coping saw
Hand or electric drill
Bits: 3mm/⅛in, 5mm/3/16in, 10mm/⅜in, countersink
Screwdrivers
Spanner
Small hammer
Bradawl
Hacksaw
Vice
Block plane or Surform
25mm/1in paintbrush

1 Mark and cut out the basic components on the ply sheet. You can draw a grid straight on to the ply if you want to get the curves absolutely right; for the base, establish the curve one side and make a template then transfer it to the other side for mirror image. Trim to the lines with the plane, and sand the surfaces.

2 Mark the screw-holes as shown, and drill 5mm/3/16in holes dead in the middle of the 12mm/½in edges. Countersink them.

Put a line of glue along the edges of back and base, hold the back upright against the back of the base and drill 3mm/7/64in pilot holes through the clearance holes; screw straight into the edge of the base. The first one is tricky, but once one screw is holding the rest is easy. It helps to make sure you have everything ready, right size drill in the chuck, and work on a flat surface at table height. Doing this on the floor is no

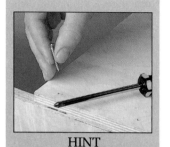

HINT
'Piloting' is drilling a small hole into the piece into which you will fix a screw. It is particularly important where the wood might otherwise split (like the ply here), or where the wood is very hard. You can break off a screw! To find the right pilot size for any screw, hold the drill bit up in front of the screw, touching it. If you can see the screw threads but not the shank, that is the right size.

HINT
Countersinking screw-holes gives room for the screw head to bury itself completely and finish flush with the surface. If you countersink deeper, you will leave a depression to take some filler and cover the screw completely; don't countersink too deep in thin material!

good. The holes must be perfectly parallel to the flat faces of the ply.

3 Fix the sides to the base and back in the same way. Fill the counter-sunk screw-head holes with water-proof filler.

STEERING BAR

4 Cut to length and shape, and drill the 75 × 25mm (3 × 1in) piece that carries the front axle: the central 10mm/⅜in hole is for the steering bolt; the holes for the rope will depend on the size of rope you have. Note that the steel axle fits under the back half of the steering bar.

Cut to length and fix the back axle mount under the seat where you judge the wheels will project up to the back corner; glue and screw it, using the six 32mm (no. 8 1¼in) bright screws; 5mm/³⁄₁₆in clearance holes in the timber and 3mm/⁷⁄₆₄in pilot holes through into the ply. Bear in mind that the axle clips will fit on this piece, and you should have a wider piece if they won't screw well home on the 50mm/2in nominal width. Also remember as you drill and screw this piece to the base that you will be screwing the clips to it, so judge where you put your screws.

5 If you cannot get decent clips to hold the axles, you can make them out of ply. Cut eight pieces from the ply left from the body pieces 28 ×

35mm/1⅛ × 1⅜in, glue them together to make pieces 24mm/1in thick, and drill through the middle the size of the axle. Drill 5mm/³⁄₁₆in clearance holes for no. 8 ×

38mm/1½in screws, and fix them to the steering bar at the front and the axle bar at the back. If you have got good clips, screw

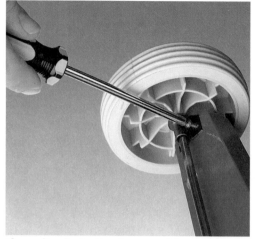

them firmly to the front and back mounts; four across the steering bar and three under the seat.

6 Now sand everything wooden, prime it, undercoat and put on two coats of non-toxic gloss.

7 With the axle clips in place, slide the steel axles in and decide the exact length you need, bearing in mind the depth of the wheels and hubs. Allow for enough washers to keep the wheels clear of the body. Cut the axles to length with the hacksaw, slide them in to the clips again, and mount washers, wheels and hubs.

8 Drill the front of the base for the 10mm/⅜in steering bolt, and pass the bolt through a small washer,

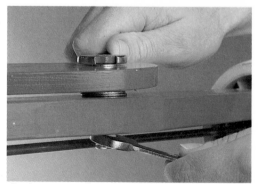

the base, another two washers, the steering bar, another washer, and the nylon locking nut or two nuts locked up against each other.

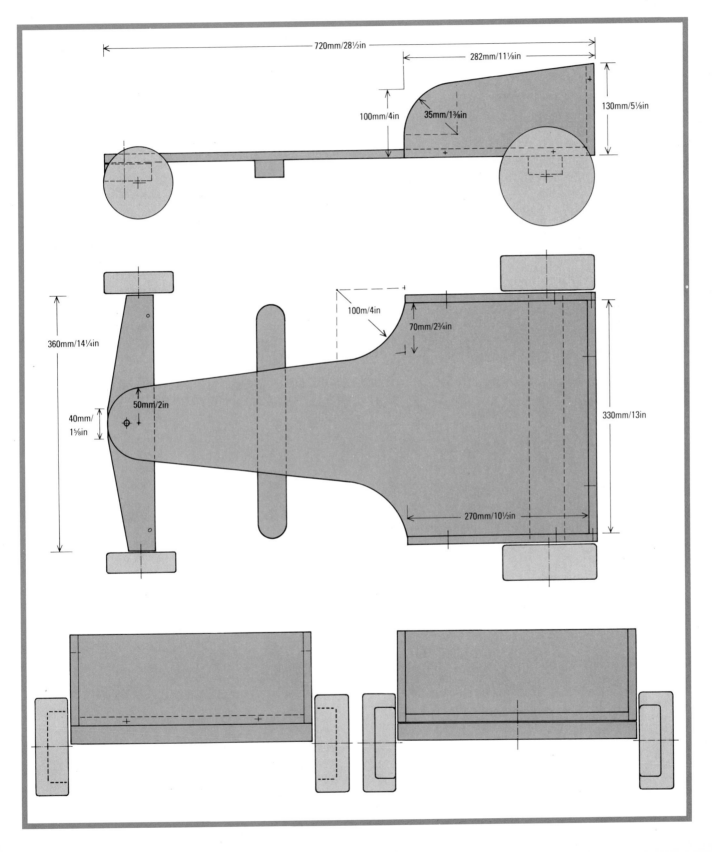

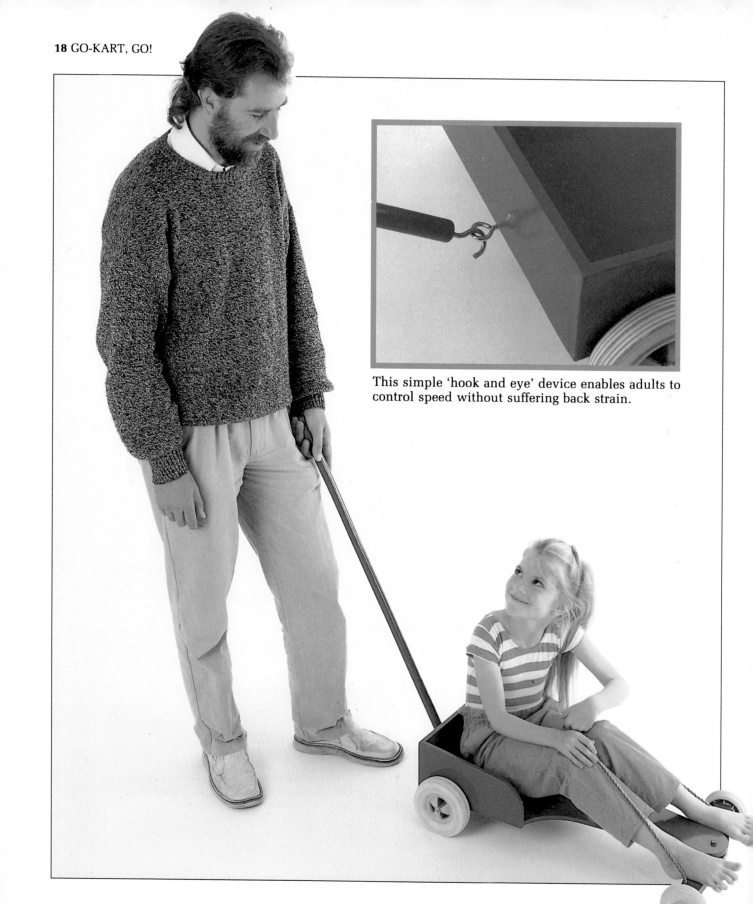

This simple 'hook and eye' device enables adults to control speed without suffering back strain.

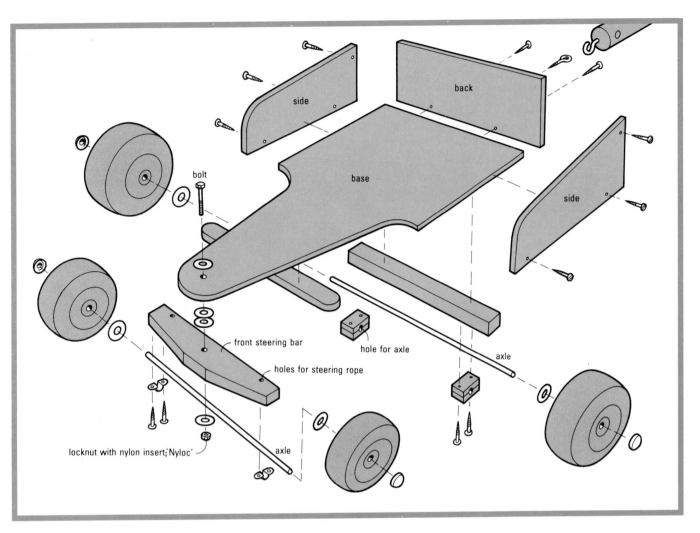

side

back

side

base

bolt

front steering bar

hole for axle

holes for steering rope

axle

locknut with nylon insert, 'Nyloc'

axle

9 Pilot drill for the screw-eye in the bottom back edge of the base, screw it in, and fix the hook in the broomstick/dowel. For strength in the weak end-grain, drill for a piece of 10mm/⅜in dowel across the broomstick's thickness just where you judge the thread of the hook will bury itself completely. Glue a dowel in the hole, and screw the hook in through that. Paint the broomstick and fix the

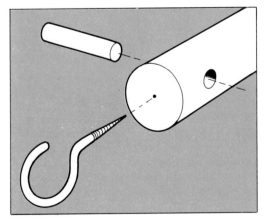

steering rope with good knots through the axle.

10 If the driver is too short to get his/ her feet on the steering bar, fix a piece of $50 \times 25mm/2 \times 1in$ timber nearer the seat for a footrest.

UP IN THE CLOUDS

This unusual toy has an intensely evocative air of the great sprint air races of the 1920s and 30s, the Schneider Trophy. It is (roughly!) modelled after the Supermarine winner, whose speed in those days, at above 200mph, was almost unheard of. Despite the everyday supersonic speeds of airplanes nowadays, there is still glory and glamour attached to these craft, and great stories of magnificent men in their flying machines will be inspired by the toy. It can hang from the ceiling or wall, and perhaps even be used in the bath – though it would need modifying to float properly.

HINT
Cut a piece of 9mm/³⁄₈in ply 168 × 40mm/6⁵⁄₈ × 1⁵⁄₈in, measuring and trimming to accurate size. Mark a diagonal line from corner to

corner and cut along it to make two 30° triangles. Cut another piece 155 × 70mm/6¹⁄₈ × 2¾in, and a third 155 × 50mm/6¹⁄₈ × 2in, and glue the 50mm/2in wide piece at right angles to the long edge of the 70mm/2¾in piece. Glue the two triangles at each end underneath, and you have the jig, the bed of which is at 30° to the horizontal.

The trickiest part of this construction is the angled drilling for the 6.5mm/¼in dowel struts which join the fuselage and floats. Other angled holes must be made for the exhaust pipes, but these should present no problem if you make up the angled drilling jig first, and go carefully, checking what you're doing at every step. The propeller is also something of a carving challenge; if you try it and it defeats you, remember that model shops will always be able to supply plastic propellers and the fittings to go with them.

FUSELAGE AND FLOATS

1 Cut the banister rail fuselage A to length; mark a centre line along the top and transfer from the gridded drawing the positions of all the holes for the exhaust pipes, struts, supercharger, etc. Cut the two floats from the 18 × 18mm/¾ × ¾in softwood, and mark centre lines along what you decide is the top; mark their fronts, and the positions of the strut holes.

2 Now comes the drilling, for which you should already have made the 30° angled jig as explained in the hint box. All the holes for the exhaust pipes are angled outwards, as are the lower holes for the undercarriage. For the floats, be sure that you are making one a mirror image of the other – this is why the fronts

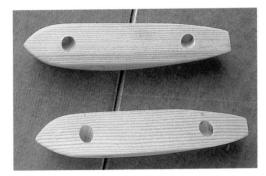

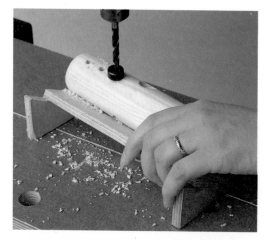

should be clearly marked, so you get the cross-strut holes on the inside of each.

Lay the fuselage with its flat face on the bed and drill vertically all the 6.5mm/¼in holes for the exhaust pipes. Turn it round and drill them on the other side. Now turn it upside down and lay it with the flat face on top parallel to the jig bed. Drill the two 6.5mm/¼in holes for the front struts only.

Put the floats in the jig and drill the front strut holes in the tops at the 30° angle — be careful to make them left and right-handed. The rear holes in the fuselage and floats for the joining struts are more tricky; cut a length of scrap and plane it to exactly 32mm/1¼in wide, and lay it under one end of the jig; this will give you the double angle you need, 12° (approximately) one

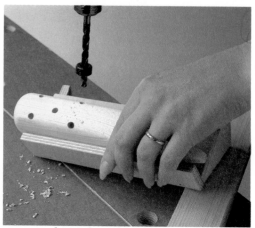

way and 30° the other. Drill with the drill vertical to the work surface and you should have no problems. If you are unsure it would be well worth cutting extra for the floats and doing a trial run.

When you have finished the angled drilling set aside the jig and drill all the other holes in the fuselage and floats for the cross-struts, supercharger mounts, propeller shaft, tail fin and wing fixings. All these are 6.5mm/¼in deep. Also bore the 18mm/¾in hole for the pilot in the top of the fuselage.

3 Transfer the fuselage tapers to a full-size gridded drawing and then to card; cut it out and mark the tapering back first. Cut that and then mark and cut the rising line from the middle towards the raised back end. Mark and cut out the flat seating for the tailplane assembly. Shape the two floats with the

MATERIALS

Ply sizes exact; softwood lengths exact, widths and thicknesses nominal

Birch faced ply		Metric			Imperial		
B Wing	1	280mm×	42mm×	9mm	11in×	1⅝in×	⅜in
C Tailplane	1	100	× 42	×9	4	×1⅝	×⅜
D Tail fin	1	50	× 42	×9	2	×1⅝	×⅜
E Exhaust fumes	1	75	× 18	×9	3	× ¾	×⅜
Banister rail							
A Fuselage	1	205	× 50	×50	8	×2	×2
First quality (FAS) softwood (pine)							
F Floats	2	108	× 18	×18	4¼×	¾	×¾
G Propeller	1	127	× 25	×12	5	×1	×½
Hardwood dowel							
H Supercharger	1	64	× 12 dia.		2½	× ½ dia.	
N Spinner	1	12	× 12 dia.		½	× ½ dia.	
I Struts	6	70	× 6.5 dia.		2¾	× ¼ dia.	
J Exhaust pipes	4	38	× 6.5 dia.		1½	× ¼ dia.	
K Exhaust pipes	2	32	× 6.5 dia.		1¼	× ¼ dia.	
L Propeller shaft	1	38	× 6.5 dia.		1½	× ¼ dia.	
M Fixings	5	12	× 6.5 dia.		½	× ¼ dia.	
P Pilot body	1	18	× 18 dia.		¾	× ¾ dia.	
Pilot head	1	18mm dia. wooden bead (¾in dia.)					
Cowling	1	50mm dia. wooden wheel (2in dia.)					
30° angle drilling jig – birch faced ply							
Angles	1	168	× 40	×9	6⅝	×1⅝	×⅜
Bed	1	155	× 70	×9	6⅛	×2¾	×⅜
Fence	1	155	× 50	×9	6⅛	×2	×⅜

Non-toxic acrylic or modelling enamel paints
Non-toxic polyurethane varnish
Glasspaper: medium, fine
Wood glue or epoxy resin glue or both

TOOLS

Tenon saw	Try square
Fret or coping and electric jigsaw	Hand or electric drill
G-cramps	Bits: 6.5mm/¼in, 7mm/⁹∕₃₂in,
Pencil, paper, tracing paper,	18mm/¾in flat bit
carbon	Bench or block plane
Steel rule, flexible rule	25mm/1in paintbrush, fine artist's
	brush

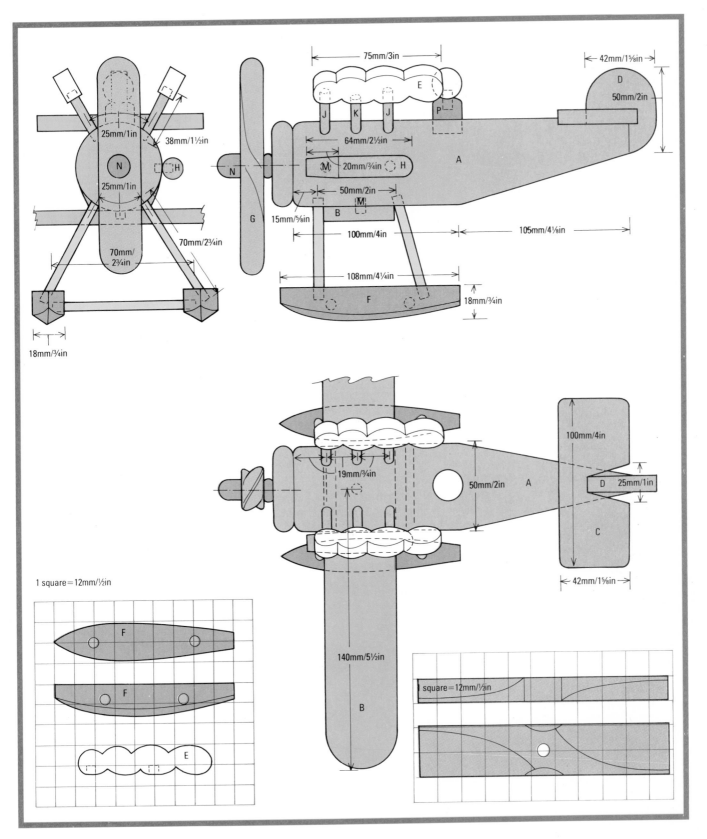

75mm/3in

42mm/1⅝in

25mm/1in

38mm/1½in

D

50mm/2in

E

J   K   J   P

N   H

M   20mm/¾in   H   A

25mm/1in

64mm/2½in

50mm/2in

105mm/4⅛in

70mm/2¾in

70mm/2¾in

M

15mm/⅝in   B

G

100mm/4in

108mm/4¼in   F   18mm/¾in

18mm/¾in

100mm/4in

19mm/¾in   50mm/2in   A   D   25mm/1in

C

42mm/1⅝in

140mm/5½in   B

1 square=12mm/½in

F

F

E

square=12mm/½in

same process – or you can measure from the printed drawing straight on to the wood with a ruler if you feel bold – and cut them out with the jig or coping saw.

Smooth with plane and glasspaper. Sand the floats and fuselage with medium and then fine glasspaper.

4 Measure and mark – from a gridded drawing or direct – the wing blank B, the tailplane C, the fin D and the exhaust fumes E on the 9mm/⅜in ply, and cut them out. Drill the wing centrally to a depth of 6.5mm/¼in with the 6.5mm/¼in drill for the fixing dowel, and the edge of the exhaust fumes after you have cut them out.

PROPELLER

5 Cut the 25 × 12mm/1 × ½in softwood exactly to 127mm/5in, and drill a 7mm/⁹⁄₃₂in hole through the

centre of the wide face. Mark out the cutting lines, transferring from a full-size gridded drawing; then draw a line diagonally from corner to corner of the endgrain at both ends, then mark a line 2mm/¹⁄₁₆ either side of that. Cut along that line and down along the marked shaped lines with the coping saw (don't use the jigsaw for this), sweeping out in a curve about 25mm/1in down from the end, and coming out

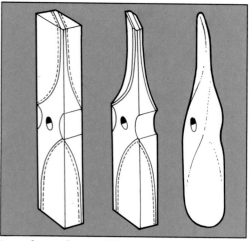

just above the middle. Do the same on the other side, and repeat it all from the other end. Cut the 'waist' either side of the hole, and clean it up with glasspaper.

FIXINGS

6 Cut all the lengths of 6.5mm/¼in dowel for the struts, supercharger mounts, and wing and tail fixings. Cut the 64mm/2½in length of 12mm/½in dowel for the supercharger and 12mm/½in of the same dowel for the propeller spinner N. Drill the mounting holes in the supercharger and the intake hole, and the mounting hole in the propeller spinner – all 6.5mm/¼in. Make the pilot peg person as explained for the racing car, with the 18mm/¾in dowel, the 18mm/¾in ball or bead, and a length of 6.5mm/¼in dowel.

Drill the centre of the 50mm/2in wooden wheel that makes the cowling.

PAINTING AND ASSEMBLY

7 Dry assemble all the parts, trimming and adjusting so that the plane sits square on the surface, the propeller spinner dowel spins easily in the nose of the fuselage, and everything is just

right. Take it all apart again, give it a final sand, then paint it with varnish and enamels in that order, or acrylic paints and varnish in that order. Mask off the areas you want different colours with tape, and rub down gently between coats of varnish with fine glasspaper. Remember if you are using ordinary wood glue for assembly not to paint the gluing areas.

8 You will find it easier to assemble the plane with tailfin and wing, supercharger and pilot as one unit, and the float structure as another.

Don't wait until the glue is dry in the floats, however, because you will almost certainly find yourself adjusting their positions. Everything fits differently when there's glue around! When the floats are on – the propeller spinner and dowel should already be glued together – fit the cowling and dowel together with some glue on the cowling; press it in position then withdraw the propeller shaft and spinner so it won't get glued in.

HINT

Ordinary wood glue (PVA, or polyvinyl acetate) is water-based, as are acrylic paints, so it will 'melt' them if you have painted a gluing area. Either mask gluing areas off, or use modelling enamels which are also non-toxic but much slower-drying. The alternative is glue with epoxy, which you have to mix but which will stick painted parts.

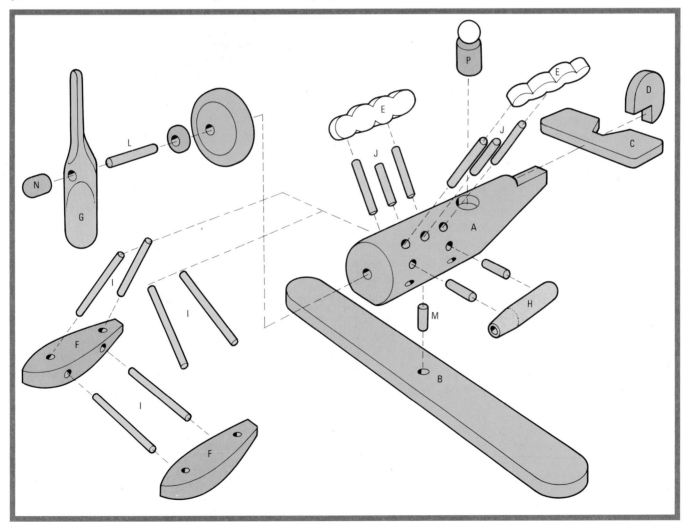

IN A SPIN

More than a little reminiscent of the traditional British pub game, bar billiards, this spinning top game has added excitement because of its central feature – the fast-spinning top in the centre of the board that knocks the swinging ball to and fro. Set the top spinning on its stand, swing the bead and see how many ping-pong balls you can knock off. The wild contortions of the swinging ball are great fun – but watch out when you first set it in motion, because the top has some power behind it and can give the ball quite a kick.

At first it seems like a game of chance, but you will find it's possible to judge the position of the little 'ear' on the edge of the top which flicks the ball around. You can devise your own competitions and variations on games that can be played, and the number of players and the scoring system can differ from game to game.

A variety of materials is needed to make the game, which is why the materials list is divided under component headings; a certain amount of ingenuity might be needed to improvise on things you can't get hold of, but there's plenty of scope for minor 're-designs'. The welding rod for the ping-pong ball stands, for instance, can be made from almost any strongish wire that takes a bend and keeps it. The 'crown cap' beer- or ale-bottle top that forms the central recess in which the top spins is another thing that could be replaced with any suitable piece of dished metal.

THE BOARD

1 Cut out the hardboard base A as a square blank, and mark the centre by squaring lines across it from side to side. It is vital that the squareness of the board is as near perfect as you can get.

Now use a steel rule to measure 73mm/ 2⅞in either side of each line where it crosses the middle of each edge; these marks should be the corners of your octagon.

Draw across the corners of your square, joining up the marks you have made, and check for accuracy and consistency; allow yourself a little tolerance, but remember

Materials

Board		Metric			Imperial		
A Base: hardboard	1	350mm×350mm×3mm			13¾in×13¾in×⅛in		
B Surround:							
softwood	8	146	× 25	×25	5¾	× 1	×1
C Stands:							
welding rod	8	175	×1.5 dia.		6⅞	×¹⁄₁₆ dia.	
D Arch:							
welding rod	1	800	× 3 dia.		31½	× ⅛ dia.	
E Swing bead	1		20 dia.		¾ dia.		
F Arch bead	1		20 dia.		¾ dia.		
G Holding beads	2		10 dia.		⅜ dia.		
H Swing string	1	400			15¾		
I Ball strings	8	140			5½		
Top							
J Shaft: wire nail	1	125			5		
K Body: birch ply	2	85	× 85	×4	3⅜	× 3⅜	×³⁄₁₆
L Weight: lead	1		74 dia.×2		3 dia.		×³⁄₃₂
M Retainer:							
panel pin	1	25			1		
N 'Ear': welding rod	1	50	× 1.5 dia		2	× ¹⁄₁₆ dia.	
Top stand							
O Cup	1	Beer bottle top					
P Body: hardboard	2	80	× 80	×3	3⅛	× 3⅛	×⅛
Top spinner							
Q Arms: birch ply	2	190	× 18	×4	7½	× ¾	×³⁄₁₆
R Body: softwood	1	75	× 40	×18	3	× 1⅝	×¾
S Rubber:							
inner tube	1	160	× 18		6¼	× ¾	
T Rod:							
hardwood dowel	1	30	× 4 dia.		1⅛	× ³⁄₁₆ dia.	
U Retainer:							
birch ply	1	40	× 15	×4	1⅝	× ⅝	×³⁄₁₆
Table tennis balls	8						
Screws							
'Twinfast' csk	19	no. 6×20			no. 6×¾		
	4	no. 6×12			no. 6×½		
	6	no. 4×12			no. 4×½		
Brass 'gimp' pins	3	18			¾		

Car body filler, PVA wood glue and/or epoxy resin glue, medium and fine glasspaper, fine steel wool, non-toxic modellers' enamels or acrylic paints and varnish, permanent black marker felt-tip pen.

you cannot then cut all the surround pieces B exactly the same.

Drill and countersink holes in the base for the screws to hold the surround pieces with a 3mm/⅛in drill.

2 Draw lines very carefully with the steel rule across from corner to corner of the octagon, going through the centre. Use the protractor to set your bevel gauge to 67½°, and mark one overlength

HINT
The bevel gauge is like an adjustable try-square; you can set it from an angle already cut on a piece of wood, or from a pencil line. Adjust it carefully then tighten the screw so it can't move. The blade slides up and down for shorter or longer lengths; judge the length you need before you set the angle. You will get the angle both sides of the stock, but in many cases you can only use the gauge one way. Always have the stock against the straight edge of the work and mark the angle off the blade.

piece of the 25×25mm/1×1in softwood across one end with the angle. Cut that very carefully and lay it along one edge of the octagonal base, matching it up with the corner-to-centre line you have drawn. If it doesn't go very well, try it on one of the other lines, or trim the end with the block plane or 25mm/1in chisel. When you're satisfied, mark off from the outside corner

350mm/13¾in

mark centre

146mm/
5¾in

73 mm/
2⅞in

and inside angled line of the other end of that section of the octagon on to the outside and inside of the surround piece: you need a really sharp pencil here, just to make the tiniest mark on the side of the surround piece, which you can then bring round to the bottom face, draw across, and cut.

Go round the whole board very carefully, cutting, marking, fitting and cutting; try to be as accurate as you can, and check all the lines you draw for the angled ends of the surround pieces with your 67½° bevel gauge. Trim for a good fit, but don't fix the surround pieces yet.

3 When all the pieces fit nicely, mark them and the base section on which they go: 'A' and 'A', 'B' and 'B' and so on. Then cut a slot in the endgrain of one end of each surround piece B to take the wire of the ping-pong ball stands C.

Drill a 1.5mm/1/16in hole – or whatever size the wire you're using for the stands is – in the bottom face of the same end of each surround piece as you have cut the slot, about 12mm/½in from the end, and chisel out a little channel from the hole to the slot.

4 Cut to length and make all the ball stands C, wrapping one end round a piece of large dowel (25mm/1in or similar) to get a good circle, and testing to see if the ping-pong balls sit in the loop well enough, but not so firmly that they won't get knocked out. Straighten the wire under the loops and trim them all to the same length if they differ, then slip the straight end of each one into its own hole in its own surround piece and bend the two right angles so it will sit in the channel

TOOLS

Pencil, paper, tracing paper, carbon paper	Block plane or Surform shaper plane
Steel rule, flexible rule, protractor, compass	Craft knife
Try-square	Metal and woodwork files
Bevel gauge	Small (4 oz) engineer's ballpein hammer
Tenon saw	Hacksaw
Coping saw and/or electric jigsaw	Centre punch
Chisels: 3mm/1/8in, 6mm/1/4in, 12mm/1/2in, 25mm/1in	Pliers
Hand or electric drill	Pincers
G-cramps	Fine artist's paintbrush
Drill bits:	25mm/1in flat brush
1mm/1/32in, 1.5mm/1/16in, 2mm/3/32in, 3mm/1/8in, 4mm/5/32in, 5mm/3/16in, 6mm/1/4in, 28mm/1⅛in	

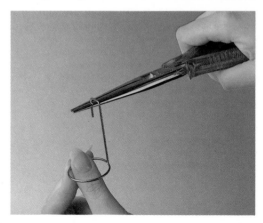

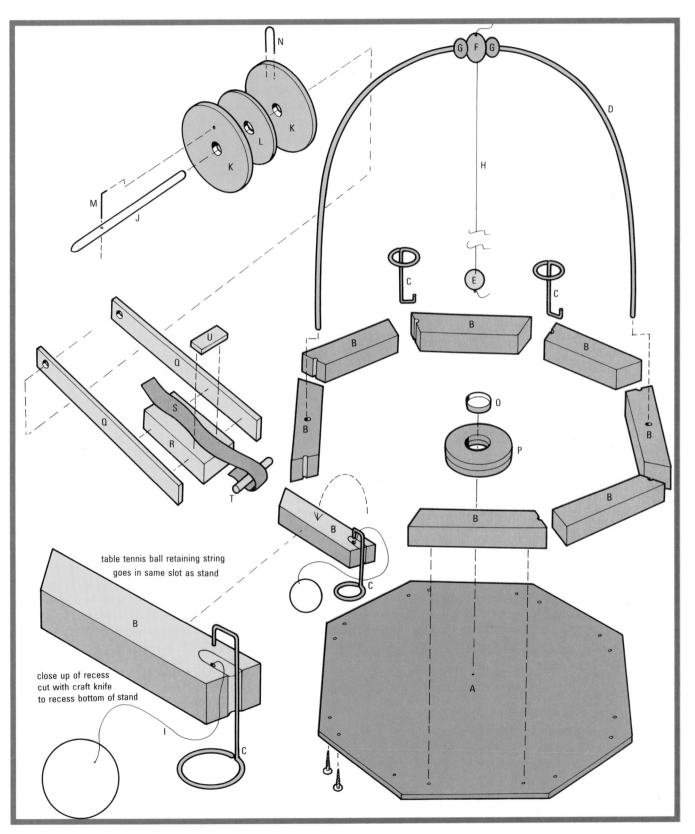

table tennis ball retaining string
goes in same slot as stand

close up of recess
cut with craft knife
to recess bottom of stand

and slot and stand up at the end of the surround. You might need to do a bit more trimming for height. Cut all the ball strings I to length, and then glue and screw the surround pieces down to their marked positions, stands and strings held in the holes and slots.

TOP STAND

5 Cut the two hardboard squares for the body P of the top stand, glue them together, and mark the centre. Now take the bottle top for the cup O and hammer out the crimps with the ballpein

hammer; you might need to improvise a little anvil here, or use another tool to get in the corners without ruining the shape.

Set the pencil and compass to 75mm/3in diameter and draw a circle on the body P, cut it out and trim it; then drill the 28mm/1⅛in hole in the middle for the cup O. You might need to adjust the size with a half-round file. Fit the cup O, then take it out again and lay the body on a flat non-stick surface – wax or grease it to make sure. Mix up some car body filler, put it in the hole, then press the cup O into the hole. Let the filler set hard, then file off sharp edges and excess filler flush with the surface with a fine file. Try not to damage the surface of the body. Glue and pin with the brass gimp pins the body to the centre of the base. File the pins off flush underneath.

ARCH AND BEADS

6 Cut the 3mm/⅛in welding rod for the arch D to length, and drill the two holding beads G with the 3mm/⅛in drill; they should sit firm on the rod without moving. Drill a 4mm/5⁄32in

hole in the arch top bead F and try that on the arch; it should spin freely. Then drill a 2mm/3⁄32in hole through the bead on its opposite axis, but offset so it doesn't foul the hole through which the arch will go.

Square a line right across the base, on top of one surround piece to its opposite, and drill 3mm/⅛in holes vertically on top of the opposite surround pieces, then slide the holding bead G, arch top bead H and the other holding bead G to the centre of the arch rod and bend it carefully, setting its 'legs' in each of the two holes. Cut the swing string H to length and drill a 2mm/

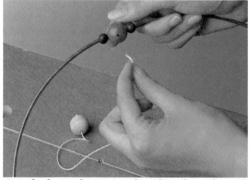

3⁄32in hole in the swing bead E, then thread the string through both beads and knot it at each end. You can adjust the 'swing length' later.

7 Attach the ball strings I to the ping-pong balls by slitting the balls slightly with a very sharp craft knife, knotting the string and pushing it in to the slot with a blob of glue.

THE TOP

8 Everything you do with the top needs to be centred and equalized, because it must balance. Cut the blanks for the top body K square, from the ply; pin them together while you work on them, like the two pieces for the stand body P. Mark the centre. Set the pencil and compass to 80mm/3⅛in, scribe the circle and cut the body round. Cut the 125mm/5in nail to 95mm/3¾in long by cutting the head off, and file the sharp end rounder and blunter. Check its diameter – it should be 4 or 5mm/5⁄32 or 3⁄16in – and drill a hole through the two body pieces K to take the nail. Put the nail in the vice and measure 22mm/7⁄8in up from the bottom blunted end, then tap a small mark with the centre punch and hammer at that point. This will give you a start for the 1.5mm/¹⁄₁₆in drill; drill a hole for the retainer panel pin M. Keep the nail in the vice while you do it.

Cut the lead weight L to 74mm/3in diameter, prise the two body pieces apart and drill four equally spaced 3mm/¹⁄₈in holes in one; slip the weight between the two and mark the centre through the hole to drill the hole for the nail. Then slide the nail through the body piece with the four holes, the weight, and the other body piece; screw them tightly together and file off the ends of the screws underneath.

Cut the head off the retainer panel pin M with pliers and bend the sharp end at right angles over the corner of a metal object like the block plane, then slip that through the hole in the nail and tap the top body down so the sharp end beds into the underside of the body. Cut and bend the 'ear' N so it makes a shape 20×6mm/³⁄₄×¹⁄₄in, and mix up some car body filler. Fill the gap between the body pieces caused by the lead weight, and push the ear into the filler while it is wet so it will set hard round the ear, which should protrude about 5mm/³⁄₁₆in.

TOP SPINNER

9 Cut the spinner arms Q exactly to size and hold them together while you drill a 6mm/¹⁄₄in hole through them both at one end, centred 12mm/¹⁄₂in from the end. Cut the body R to size, and drill 3mm/¹⁄₈in holes in the other ends of the arms from the single hole to screw them to the body. Glue and screw one to

the body then set the other up on the other edge with the top shaft J going through them both so you get them lined up accurately. Tap the screws in to give them a start so the arm won't move while you

screw it up with no. 4×12mm/¹⁄₂in screws.

Now cut the rubber S, rod T and retainer U, and drill two 3mm/⁷⁄₆₄in holes in the retainer. Wind the rubber round the rod and position it held by the retainer so the end of the rubber comes to about 30mm/1¹⁄₈in from the holes for the top shaft J without being stretched. Tap the screws through into the side of the spinner body and screw them up tight.

10 Get someone to hold the top in the stand vertically while you adjust the knots on the swing string H so the swing bead E will just catch the ear of the top as it spins round. Cut off the waste bits of string. Before you paint everything, check that it all works; hold the swing ball out of play while you load the top in the spinner and wind the rubber round it; hold it firmly with both hands while your partner holds the swing bead 'out of play', and set it in the stand, then let go of the rubber and lift the spinner off the top shaft.

If it's too difficult to take off without disturbing the equilibrium of the top, you might need to make the holes in the spinner arms bigger. Let your partner let go of the swing bead, and you're away.

11 When everything works OK, take the bits and pieces apart that will come, or just be careful not to let different coloured paints bleed into each other, either by masking off or letting one area dry before you do the next. Use modeller's enamels over a base coat of varnish, or acrylic paints which you then protect with two coats of varnish on top.

Sand everything carefully before you

paint with medium then fine glasspaper, and rub down lightly between coats. Polish the metal parts with fine steel wool, and draw the numbers on the ping-pong balls with permanent black marker.

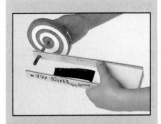

HINT
To use the top spinner you must insert the rod of the top through the holes in the end of the spinner, and wind the rubber tightly and

neatly around the rod as far as it will go.

Now, holding the roll of rubber in place with finger and thumb, position the top above the centre of the game board, and let go of the rubber whilst lifting the spinner off the shaft of the top.

HORSE AND CART

Another traditional favourite, this horse with his own cart and cargo of bricks is designed both to be pulled along and sat upon – by smaller children! He naturally has the colour scheme of a shire horse, or just an old grey workhorse – so why not experiment with a few white markings as well? It's best in this case to remind yourself of how white tends to appear in the coat of a grey horse by looking at photographs. Co-ordination skills will improve as the child attempts to manoeuvre the cart around corners.

The cart is designed to carry 15 bricks in rows of three across, so bear in mind that the length and even the width of the base should be measured against your bricks. This is why we suggest making the bricks before the cart! 'Nominal' sizes for the timber concerned are given in the materials list, but remember that it is only by accurate measuring of the wood once it's on the bench in front of you that you will know exactly how wide and how long to make the cart base. Take your list and a tape rule to the timber yard when you buy. The length on the drawing is based on bricks of 45 × 45mm in /$1^{13}/_{16}$ × $1^{13}/_{16}$in, which is approximately the size that 50 × 50mm/2 × 2in will come out after it has been planed in the timber yard.

The accurate fit of the head into the body is dependent on careful use of the chisel. It's best to have a few chisels – say 12mm /$^1/_2$in, 19mm /$^3/_4$in and 25mm /1in, but if you only want to invest in one, the 19mm /$^3/_4$in size is probably the most useful. It so happens that the wide recess you need to

TOOLS	
Pencil	Screwdriver
Steel rule and flexible rule	Hand or electric drill
Tracing and carbon paper	Drill bits:
Tenon saw	3mm/$^1/_8$in, 5mm/$^3/_{16}$in, 6.5mm/
Coping saw or electric jigsaw	$^1/_4$in, 25mm/1in flat bit – or
G-cramps	25mm/1in bit for carpenter's
Try square	brace
Marking gauge	25mm/1in paintbrush
19mm/$^3/_4$in chisel	Fine artist's brush
Mallet and hammer	

cut in this particular job for the fit of the head in the body would be neatest cut with a 25mm/1in!

THE HEAD

1 Cut the two pieces for the head A to length, and examine the end-grain. Stick them together to make the thickness; make sure they go together with the growth rings curving away at the ends and towards each other in the middle.

Wood 'moves' as if to flatten out the rings, and if this happens the edge joints will not separate. Draw out your full-size grid and the shape of the head on it, then transfer that via tracing and carbon paper to the wood and cut it out with a jigsaw or coping saw. The grain should be from neck to nose, and the notch at the back of the neck as neat and square as possible. Mark out here with a square and cut this corner off with a tenon saw.

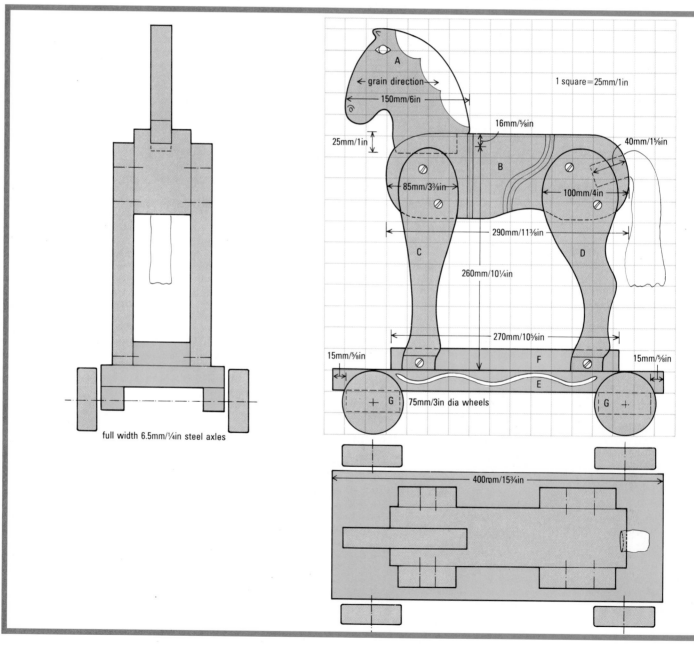

full width 6.5mm/¼in steel axles

grain direction

150mm/6in

1 square=25mm/1in

25mm/1in

16mm/⅝in

40mm/1⅝in

85mm/3⅜in

100mm/4in

290mm/11⅜in

260mm/10¼in

270mm/10⅝in

15mm/⅝in

15mm/⅝in

75mm/3in dia wheels

400mm/15¾in

MARKING OUT

2 Cut the horse's body B to length and perfectly square; don't shape it until you have cut the slot for the head and marked the position of the legs.

Set the marking gauge to 16mm/⅝in and scribe a short line from the top edge, front and back, on both sides where the tops of the legs will be. Then measure back from the top front square edge of the body 86mm/3⅜in and square a line across; this is the back of the head slot. Measure the exact thickness of the head (it will probably be about 40–42mm/1¹¹⁄₁₆in), then establish the centre line of the body in the head slot area and measure half the head's thickness either side. Set the gauge to the distance from the outside edge of the body to the mark that shows the head's thick-

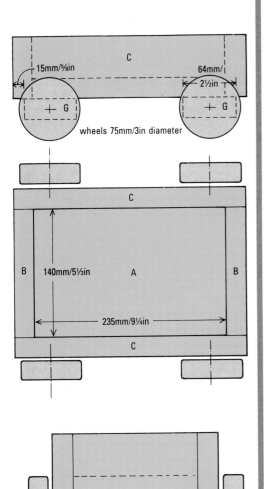

15mm/⅝in   C   64mm/ 2½in

+ G   + G

wheels 75mm/3in diameter

B   140mm/5½in   A   B

C

235mm/9¼in

C

MATERIALS

lengths exact; widths/thicknesses nominal.

First quality (FAS) softwood (pine)

Horse		Metric			Imperial		
A Head	2	150mm×	150mm×	25mm	6in×	6in×	1in
B Body	1	290	×100	×75	11⅜×	4	×3
C Front legs	2	260	× 75	×25	10¼×	3	×1
D Back legs	2	260	×100	×25	10¼×	4	×1
E Lower base	1	400	×150	×25	15¾×	6	×1
F Upper base	1	270	× 75	×50	10⅝×	3	×2
G Axle bearers	8	64	× 25	×25	2½×	1	×1
Bricks	15	50	× 50	×50	2	× 2	×2
Cart							
A Base	1	245	×150	×25	9⅝×	6	×1
B Ends	2	150	× 75	×25	6	× 3	×1
C Sides	2	295	× 75	×25	11⅝×	3	×1
Steel axles (horse)	2	175	×6.5 dia.		6⅞×	¼ dia.	
Steel axles (cart)	2	200	×6.5 dia.		7⅞×	¼ dia.	
Spring washer/dome							
cap hubs	8	6.5mm internal dia.			¼in internal dia.		
Steel washers	17		6.5mm internal dia.		¼in internal dia.		
Screws:							
Brass csk	12	no. 8 × 38			no. 8 × 1½		
Steel csk	18	no. 8 × 32			no. 8 × 1¼		
Brass screw cups	12	no. 8					
Panel pins		32mm			1¼in		
Wooden wheels	8	75mm dia.			3in dia.		
Cup hook (straight)	1						
Screw eye	2	8mm internal dia.			⅜in internal dia.		
Ball white string	1						
Nylon rope		450mm×6mm dia.			18in×¼in dia.		

Non-toxic acrylic or modelling enamel paints, and polyurethane varnish (clear gloss)

HINT
A marking gauge is used against an edge to scribe a line a set distance from that edge. You need a good steel rule to set it accurately; get it as near as you can, tighten up 2/3rds, then make marks to test on scrap. If it is too much, tap the pin end lightly on the bench and test again; if too little, tap the other end. Fully tighten it when it's dead right.

ness, and gauge a line from each side of the body, running from the squared-across mark at the back of the slot you will cut to the front edge of the body. You have marked out for the slot that will take the neck. Square a line across the front end of the body 25mm/1in down from the top, and run the gauge lines down the front edge to that mark. This is the slot's depth.

3 Now make a mark 12.5mm/½in inside the gauged lines that show where the slot will be, and set the gauge from the outside face of the body-piece to that mark. Gauge another line along in the slot area, and repeat from the other side. This is the centre-line of the 25mm/1in bit or flat bit; mark off centres so that the holes you will drill will just overlap, and do it the other side. The holes

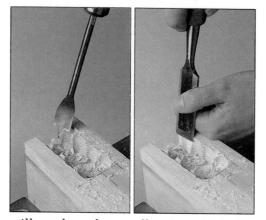

will overlap substantially across the body; make sure that the 25mm/1in holes will not cross the lines you have gauged and marked for the slot. Mark the drill to 25mm/1in with tape, and drill out the holes. Now all you have to do is clean out the slot to the lines with a *sharp* chisel.

Make the bottom flat and the sides vertical, and test-fit the neck continually. It should be a good tight fit, and the notch at the back of the neck should seat perfectly.

THE LEGS

4 It is still not time to cut the shape of the body. Cut the legs exactly to length and perfectly square at the ends, and transfer the hole positions for the screws onto the oblong leg-blanks.

Square a line down from the top of the body 100mm/4in from the back end, and 86mm/3⅜in in from the front. These lines

mark the inside positions of the legs before shaping. Drill 5mm/³⁄₁₆in clearance holes for no. 8 screws in the marked positions on the legs, put screws loosely in the holes, then line up the tops of the still-square leg-blanks with the lines you have gauged down from the top of the body, and their inside long edges with the lines you have just made. Tap the screws sharply with a hammer to mark the exact hole positions on the body.

5 At last you can shape the body and the legs. Mark out the curves front, back and underneath the body from your full-sized gridded drawing, and cut them with a jigsaw or coping saw; do the same for the legs. Drill the 25mm/1in hole 40mm/1⅝in deep for the horse's tail.

Sand all the components thoroughly, perhaps using the chisel to shape the features on the head – nose, ears, etc. Round off all the corners except the edges where the head fits into the body.

6 Now glue the horse up. Spread glue carefully, not too thick, not too thin, all over the head slot; tap the head into position with the mallet, making sure it seats well. Clean off excess glue with a chisel and damp cloth.

Pilot drill the hole-positions for the leg screws in the body with the 3mm/⅛in bit, then spread glue on the top of each leg in turn where it meets the body, set the screw-cups on the screws and the screws loosely in their holes, and poke them through to find their positions on the body. Screw them up, but not too tight; when you have got all four legs on, stand the horse up on a flat surface and see if and where he rocks. If slight movement in the legs will straighten him up, you can adjust them against the screws then tighten them up; if there is really drastic instability, see 'hint' on p.38.

7 Cut the two base components E and F exactly to length and square. Set the gauge to the centre line of each, and mark the lower one E about where the top one F will sit on it; gauge the centre line of top base F on its bottom corners. Mark the position of the front from the drawing, then drill two 5mm/³⁄₁₆in holes through the lower base E diagonally across the area where the upper base will go. Spread glue on the bottom of the upper base, lay it down on E matching up the centre lines and the back-to-front position line, and hold it with G-cramps while you drill 3mm/⅛in holes through the existing screw-holes into the upper base; screw through to hold the two firmly together.

Drill pilot holes for the screw-eyes in the centre of each end of the base.

8 Cut all the axle bearers – you might as well do them for the cart now as well – and drill 5mm/³⁄₁₆in clearance holes at each end of each. Mark the

base 15mm/⅝in in from each end on the bottom, and the sides of the axle bearers exactly in the middle of their length; then glue, clamp, pilot-drill and screw them to the edges of the bottom of the base, lining up their 'outside' ends with the 15mm/⅝in marks. Use the 32mm/1¼in steel screws.

Drill 6.5mm/¼in holes through the centre-marks on the sides, then square a line across to the other axle-bearer and over on to its side so you can drill the other

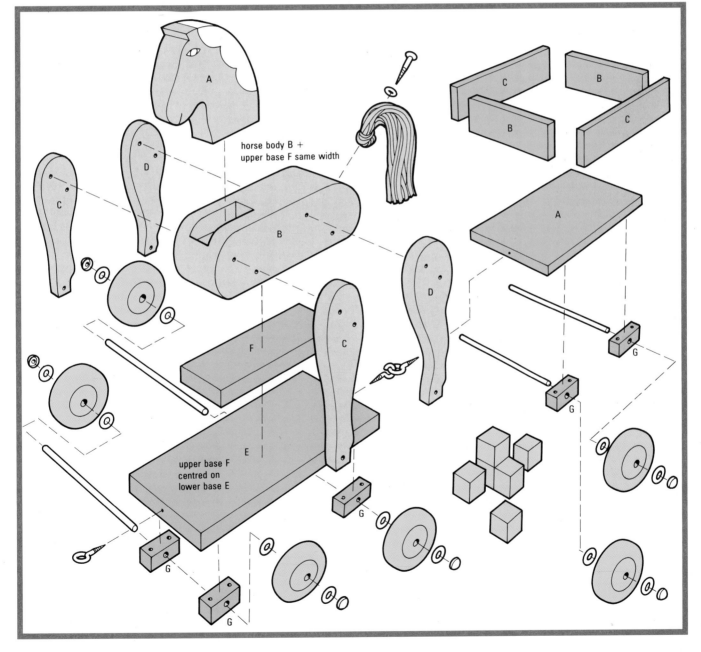

horse body B +
upper base F same width

upper base F
centred on
lower base E

HINT
If a set of legs are out of
level, block them up
until there is no rocking
on a flat surface; set a
pencil and compass to
the widest gap you can
find, and mark off from
the surface to all the
other legs. Cut and trim
to the lines you have
made.

hole exactly square across the base. Be careful about this; you can enlarge the holes slightly when you fit the axles, but you do need to be accurate.

9 Now you have the base, the bearers, the horse; but not the cart or the bricks. Take your 50 × 50mm/2 × 2in length for the bricks, and measure it on both short dimensions; then decide the length you need to cut to make as near perfect cubes as possible. Mark one out, squaring a line all the way round, cut it, trim it and get it as good as possible; then mark this as your master and use it to mark out all the others. You have 15 to do, but make every effort to get them as right as possible, because the eye picks up discrepancies.

When you have got them all to your satisfaction, line up three across and measure them, add 6mm/¼in, and that is the width of the base of your cart. The 150mm/6in timber you have bought should be big enough, but you might have to cut the width down a bit. Similarly, line up five of the bricks and measure them all across; this gives you the length of your cart base, plus you must add 9mm/⅜in.

Now cut the base A to size and square it up, cut the ends B to length exactly the width of the base, and cut the sides C the length of the base plus twice the thickness of the ends. Sand the inside faces of all the pieces.

10 Glue and cramp the ends of the cart to the base, then glue and cramp the sides to the edges of the base and the ends of the ends. Make sure it all lines up as square as possible, but if there are discrepancies you can plane and sand them away when the glue is dry.

Drill, mark, glue, pilot, and drill for axles and screw the axle bearers to the base in exactly the same way as you did for the horse.

11 When the glue is dry, give everything a final sand, and pay particular attention to removing hardened excess glue with the chisel. Paint the pieces, having first made sure you have marked and masked the parts which are to be glued to each other – the legs and base of the horse. Use the gridded drawings to mark out the mane, saddle, and so on; use the colours you see in the photograph – or

exercise your imagination! Paint the basic colours with two coats, let them dry then do the details; when all the paint is dry, glue, pilot and screw the horse's legs to the base – not forgetting the screw cups. Varnish the bricks with two coats.

12 Drill the wheels for the 6.5mm/¼in steel axles, cut the axles to length, push them through the axle bearers – enlarge the holes with a drill if you need to – and fit washers, wheels, washers, and the spring washer/dome cap hubs in that order.

Screw the cup hook into the back of the horse base, one of the eyes into the front of the cart base, and the other into the front of the horse base. Now attach the rope.

13 The final touch is the tail. Wind the string between your elbow and hand about 25 times, cut it and tie

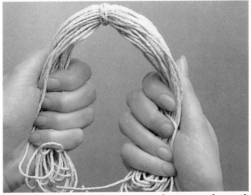

it in the middle, then pour glue into the tail hole, fold the tail in two, and push it into the hole. Tamp it in with a piece of 12mm/

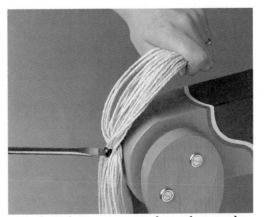

½in dowel. Put a screw through a washer and screw it in deep in the hole for extra strength.

DREAM COTTAGE

No collection of wooden toys would be complete without the doll's house, an eternal classic like the hobby horse or wooden train. This one doesn't aim for the complication and obsessive detail of the collectors' pieces; it is a real house for ordinary everyday dolls. The colour scheme gives it an olde-worlde air, in fact, but inside there is a lot of scope for making it much more modern and up-to-date; which is why the 'open riser' staircase is already installed. A piece of craftsmanship like this will be passed on through generations of children, so it is worth taking your time while making it, ensuring that each little detail is as near-perfect as possible.

On the ground floor there are two spacious rooms which need only the appropriate furniture to become kitchen/diner and cosy sitting room. Upstairs there are three compartments just waiting to be converted into bedrooms and bathroom. If the price of shop-bought doll's house furniture

TOOLS

Pencil, paper, tracing paper, carbon paper
Steel rule, flexible rule
Try-square
Electric jigsaw
Coping or fret saw
Tenon saw
Gent's or jeweller's saw
Bevel gauge
Marking gauge

Block plane or Surform shaper plane
Chisels: 3mm/⅛in, 6mm/¼in, 12mm/½in, 19mm/¾in
Hand or electric drill
Drill bits: 1.5mm/1⁄16in, 3mm/⅛in, 5mm/3⁄16in, 6.5mm/¼in, 12mm/½in, countersink
Bradawl
Half-round fine cut file or wood rasp

Screwdrivers
Pliers
Pincers
'Junior' hacksaw
Fine metalworker's file
Craft knife or scalpel
Permanent black felt-tip marker
Paintbrushes: no. 6 sable, 12mm/½in flat brush, 25mm/1in flat brush

MATERIALS

3mm/1/8in Hardboard/Masonite (total sheet size 1800×1200×3mm, 72×48×1/8in)

		Metric			Imperial		
A Ground floor	1	600mm	×294mm	×3mm	23 5/8in	×11 5/8in	×1/8in
B Outer walls	2	400	×300	×3	15 3/4	×11 7/8	×1/8
C Back	1	630	×400	×3	24 3/4	×15 3/4	×1/8
D Upper floor	1	620	×294	×3	24 3/8	×11 5/8	×1/8
E Upper ceiling	1	598	×240	×3	23 1/2	× 9 1/2	×1/8
F Roof	2	630	×230	×3	24 3/4	× 9	×1/8
G Roof gables	2	300	×150	×3	11 7/8	× 6	×1/8
H Stair treads	9	73	× 30	×3	2 7/8	× 1 3/16	×1/8
I Chimney sides	4	134	× 70	×3	5 1/4	× 2 3/4	×1/8
J Chimney top	1	70	× 64	×3	2 3/4	× 2 1/2	×1/8
K Porch roofs	2	100	× 35	×3	4	× 1 3/8	×1/8
L Porch gables	2	137	× 67	×3	5 3/8	× 2 5/8	×1/8

4mm/3/16in best birch plywood (total sheet size 1200×700×4mm, 48×27 5/8×3/16in)

M Front	1	600	× 370	×4	23 5/8	× 14 5/8	×3/16
N 1st inside wall	1	392	× 284	×4	15 3/8	× 11 1/8	×3/16
O 2nd inside wall	1	187	× 284	×4	7 3/8	× 11 1/8	×3/16
P Ridge tiles	1	535	× 30	×4	21 1/16	× 1 3/16	×3/16
Q Banister rail	1	90	× 90	×4	3 1/2	× 3 1/2	×3/16
R Stair strings (sides)	2	310	× 70	×4	12 1/4	× 2 3/4	×3/16
S Top window surrounds	2	100	× 98	×4	4	× 3 7/8	×3/16
T Bottom window surrounds	2	125	× 109	×4	5	× 4 1/4	×3/16
U Central window surround	1	80	× 80	×4	3 1/8	× 3 1/8	×3/16
V Porch bargeboards	2	110	× 28	×4	4 3/8	× 1 1/8	×3/16
W Porch ridge post	1	67	× 22	×4	2 5/8	× 7/8	×3/16
X Chimney top ridge	2	84	× 12	×4	3 1/4	× 1/2	×3/16
	2	78	× 12	×4	3 1/8	× 1/2	×3/16
Y Nameboard	1	62	× 10	×4	2 1/2	× 3/8	×3/16

First quality (FAS) softwood (pine). Lengths exact; widths and thicknesses nominal

Crosspieces	3	600	× 25	×13	23 5/8	× 1	×1/2
Pillars	2	373	× 25	×13	14 3/4	× 1	×1/2
Bargeboards:							
chimney end	2	238	× 25	×13	9 3/8	× 1	×1/2
ridge post end	2	222	× 25	×13	8 3/4	× 1	×1/2
Porch inners	3	29	× 25	×13	1 1/8	× 1	×1/2
Porch brackets	2	40	× 30	×13	1 5/8	× 1 3/16	×1/2
Roof ridge supports	3	45	× 25	×13	1 3/4	× 1	×1/2
Ridge post	1	105	× 25	×25	4 1/8	× 1	×1
Fireplace	2	65	× 25	×13	2 1/2	× 1	×1/2
	1	75	× 25	×13	3	× 1	×1/2

daunts you, why not try making your own out of covered cotton reels and matchboxes, sea shells, corks – anything! Postage stamps make excellent pictures to adorn the living room wall.

The painting of the house is quite a challenge, and it would pay you to take careful note of the colour schemes and draw out guidelines for yourself, either on full-size blanks or on the primed wood, to make sure everything fits, that all the roof tiles end up the same size, and so on. It is particularly important to prime with white emulsion (latex US) paint, because the many small areas of different colours will bleed into each other if they are painted straight on to the absorbent wood.

None of the components are particularly difficult to cut, but go through the drawings carefully to make sure you understand where all the slots are placed for the locating of the walls and floors. The roof is detachable, the front swings open, and the whole thing is screwed together so that it can be dry-assembled before painting. Since there are a number of very small components to be cut, you will find a 'gent's saw', or even a jeweller's saw, very useful, with their many small teeth and extra-fine cut.

Please also note that although the softwood battens are stated as 25 × 13mm/1 × 1/2in on the cutting list, their lengths are based on the normal assumption that they will finish to about 22mm/7/8in wide and slightly less than 13mm/1/2in thick. Check with your rule and adjust the lengths accordingly for a good tight fit.

MAIN STRUCTURE

1 Measure, mark and accurately cut and trim the floor A, walls B and back C. Cut the slots in exactly the right positions and cut the battens for the pieces, noting the exact lengths both from the cutting list and by checking with your own dimensions.

The procedure for battening is; drill three or four 5mm/3/16in holes in the batten according to length, countersink them, then lay glue on their backs, lay them in place and tap the sharp points of the no. 6 × 12mm/1/2in screws into the hardboard. Screw up; the screw should bite. If it does not, you will have to pilot drill every hole with a 3mm/ ⅛in for the no. 8 screws — a real chore with this many holes, so try the bradawl first to give a hole for the screw to start. Then likewise drill and screw the walls to the floor with the no. 8 × 25mm/ 1in screws, and the back to the walls and floor with 10 no. 6 × 20mm/¾in screws.

Throughout the construction of the house, remember to countersink the holes you drill — particularly where the screw-heads must finish flush with the surface. Fill all countersink recesses with car body filler before you paint.

2 Cut the front pillars and the three crosspieces to length from the 25 × 13mm/1 × ½in softwood, and measure, mark and cut with saw and 3mm/ ⅛in chisel the slots in them for internal walls. These must be 5mm/³⁄₁₆in deep and 220mm/8⅝in from each end; they are cut in the 13mm/½in face of the top front piece, and in the 25mm/1in face of the top back piece and upper floor support piece. The upper floor support piece also has notches cut out of the ends to fit round the vertical side pillars when the floor is in place; these are 12mm/½in down the length of the piece and 5mm/³⁄₁₆in into its width.

Drill, countersink, glue and fix them to their respective positions on the inside front edges of the walls B with the no. 8 × 25mm/1in screws; note you can screw through the outer battens and wall into the pillars, or through the pillars and wall into the outer battens.

It will be easier to cut the hinge recesses in the pillars with your chisel before you fix them. They are 47mm/1⅞in

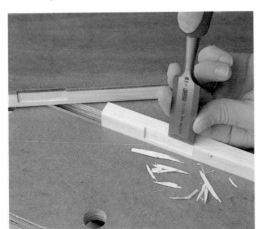

MATERIALS

Battens:		**Metric**			**Imperial**			
Floor	2	556mm×	25mm	×13mm	21⅞in×	1	in×	½in
	2	354 ×	25	×13	14 ×	1	×	½
	1	310 ×	25	×13	12¼ ×	1	×	½
Sides	4	400 ×	25	×13	15¾ ×	1	×	½
	2	256 ×	25	×13	10⅛ ×	1	×	½
Upper ceiling	1	624 ×	25	×13	24⅝ ×	1	×	½
Front	1	600 ×	25	×13	24½ ×	1	×	½
	2	326 ×	25	×13	12⅞ ×	1	×	½
	2	260 ×	25	×13	10¼ ×	1	×	½
Roof gables	4	210 ×	25	×13	8¼ ×	1	×	½
Chimney	4	134 ×	25	×13	5¼ ×	1	×	½
	1	64 ×	25	×13	2½ ×	1	×	½

Hardwood dowel							
Balusters	13	70	×	6.5 dia.	2¾	×	¼ dia.
Stair supports	3	54	×	6.5 dia.	2⅛	×	¼ dia.
Extra for general							
use		200	×	6.5 dia.	8	×	¼ dia.
Chimney	1	50	×	38 dia.	2	×	1½ dia.
Chimney peg	1	35	×	12 dia.	1⅜	×	½ dia.

Ridge post ball:				
wooden ball			20 dia.		¾ dia.
Door handle:				
yellow bead			12 dia.		½ dia.
Door latch:				
22g brass	1	25	×	25	1	×	1
Csk head bolt,	1	M3	×	25	⅛ Whitworth ×1
nuts, washers				

Windows:									
perspex	2	100	×	80	×3	4	×	3⅛	×⅛
	2	80	×	80	×3	3⅛	×	3⅛	×⅛
	1	60	×	60	×3	2⅜	×	2⅜	×⅛
Brass hinges	2	50				2			

Screws:
Bright zinc plated twinfast thread (ie chipboard screws with sharp points and thread)

17	no. 8 ×	25	no. 8 ×	1
8	no. 8 ×	38	no. 8 ×	1½
1	no. 8 ×	50	no. 8 ×	2
28	no. 6 ×	20	no. 6 ×	¾
2	no. 6 ×	25	no. 6 ×	1
approx.100	no. 6 ×	12	no. 6 ×	½
Brass csk: 17	no. 4 ×	12	no. 4 ×	½

Panel pins	12, 16, 25	½, ⅝, 1

Car body filler
Medium and fine glasspaper
Brass wire; 5mm/³⁄₁₆in dia. white and black self-adhesive decorative surface paper ('Fablon'), white carpet tape
Paints: non-toxic modeller's enamels or acrylics: crimson, signal red, brown, yellow ochre, deep green, black, white; emulsion (water-based latex US): brown, white; Non-toxic polyurethane varnish (spray can preferable)
Wood glue and epoxy resin glue

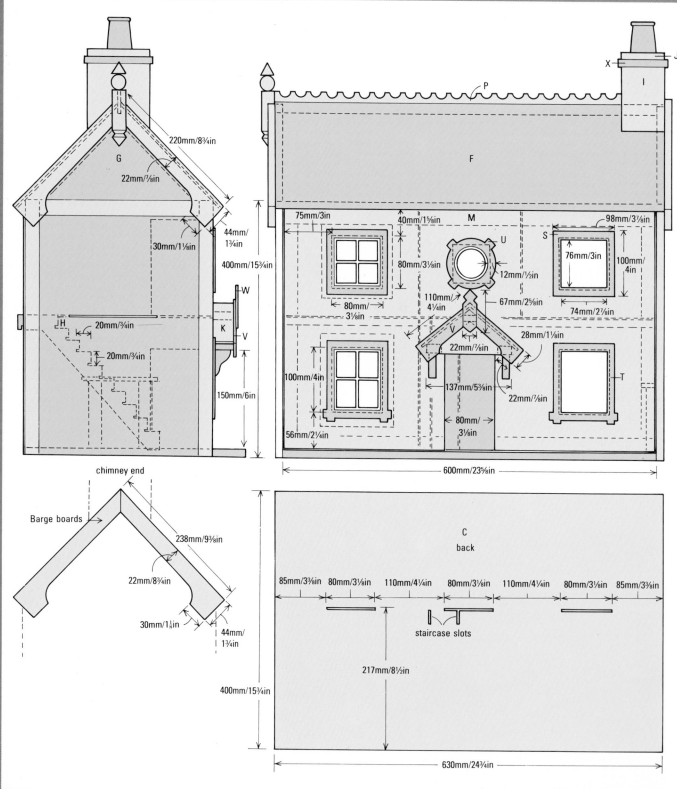

220mm/8¾in

22mm/⅞in

G

44mm/1¾in

30mm/1⅛in

400mm/15¾in

W

H

20mm/¾in

20mm/¾in

K

V

150mm/6in

chimney end

Barge boards

238mm/9⅜in

22mm/8¾in

30mm/1⅛in

44mm/1¾in

P

F

J

X

I

75mm/3in

40mm/1⅝in

M

98mm/3⅞in

S

U

80mm/3⅛in

76mm/3in

100mm/4in

12mm/½in

67mm/2⅝in

74mm/2⅞in

80mm/3⅛in

110mm/4¼in

28mm/1⅛in

V

22mm/⅞in

100mm/4in

137mm/5⅜in

22mm/⅞in

T

56mm/2¼in

80mm/3⅛in

600mm/23⅝in

C
back

85mm/3⅜in 80mm/3⅛in 110mm/4¼in 80mm/3⅛in 110mm/4¼in 80mm/3⅛in 85mm/3⅜in

staircase slots

217mm/8½in

400mm/15¾in

630mm/24¾in

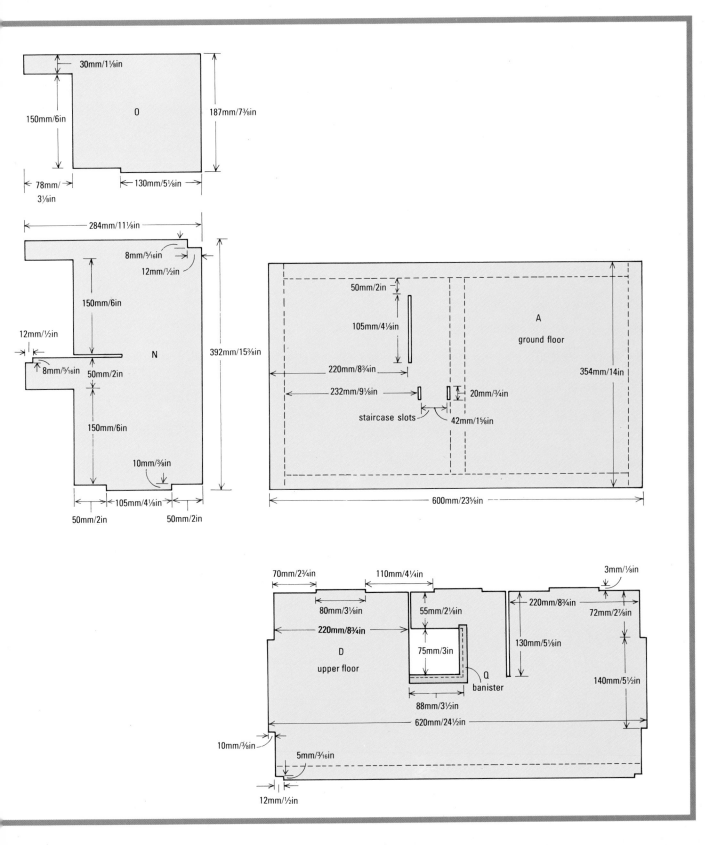

down and up from the top and bottom of the left-hand pillar as you face the house.

3 Drill, countersink and screw-fix the top front crosspiece to the tops of the pillars with no. 8 × 38mm/ 1½in screws; note you must miss the other screws already there, and remember also

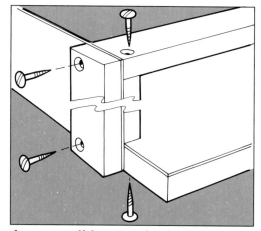

that you will be using hinge screws near the top and bottom of the left-hand pillar.

Fix the back top crosspiece to both the sides and back with no. 8 and no. 6 × 20mm/¾in screws.

UPPER FLOOR AND INTERNAL WALLS

4 The steps up to now have all been so you can see that everything fits. Now you must measure, mark and cut from the hardboard and ply the upper floor D and the two internal walls, the full-height one N and the half-height one O.

Cut out the full-size blanks first, trim them absolutely square, then mark them all out carefully for the notches, slots and holes, double-checking by adding up your measurements different ways, and by holding uncut pieces up against the structure.

Cut all the external notches with straight-bladed saws like the tenon or gent's saw; for internal holes like the one for the stairwell, do as much as you can with the straight-bladed saw then go over to the coping or fret-saw. Drill, glue and screw-fix the upper floor support piece across the front under edge of the floor, making sure the notches in both marry up with each other and with the pillars on either side of the structure.

BANISTER

5 Cut out the full-size blank as shown on the drawing for the banister Q, having measured and marked carefully on the 4mm/³⁄₁₆in ply, and mark the positions of all the balusters with the bradawl. Drill 6.5mm/¼in holes in each end of the right angle, and cut all the balusters from the 6.5mm/¼in dowel; now lay the banister rail Q carefully against the stairwell hole on the upper floor D in the position it will be, and mark through the centres of the two holes you have drilled on to the floor with the bradawl.

Drill holes exactly on those marks, then use two of the dowels you have cut to go through both banister Q and floor D, holding the banister in position but flat on the floor. Now drill through the marks you have made on the banister, through the floor as well. This way the holes are lined up and the balusters will be vertical. Set all the dowels into the banister then the floor, and check everything lines up nicely. Don't glue them yet.

STAIRS

6 Mark and cut out the two full-size blanks for the stair sides – the strings R (strings is the proper joinery term!) – and clamp them together to trim them up perfectly square. Then draw up a full size grid, and draw out the string on it with all its cutaways; you can trace that on to card and cut it out, then just transfer the lines by drawing round it on to the ply, or you can mark and measure it all out full size. If you do the latter, get a good idea of how the top and bottom edges of the strings lie on the blank, then set the bevel gauge to the angle between the long edge of the blank and the line of the top and bottom edges of the string, and you can then keep the same angle for all the steps, to avoid a higgledy-piggledy staircase.

Mark the positions of the three holes for the dowel supports and drill through them while the two blanks are held together, then cut the 54mm/2⅛in dowel supports and use those to keep the strings together while you cut them out. You will have to work out very carefully what cuts will be the ones that separate the strings from the blank; try to keep it all in one piece as long as you can.

J

X I I X
X I I X
X I

F
P
G
G
F

E

Fablon
Fablon
glass
window surround
S

C
N
O
Q
B
M

D

B

A

R
R
R
H

K
L
L
K
V
W
Y

12mm/½in
bead

door knob & latch

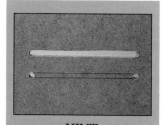

HINT

If you have to cut a slot in the centre of a board, mark it out and drill just smaller than its width at each end – or in the case of a large hole, at each corner. Detach the blade of the coping saw from one end and slip it through the hole, then fix it back in the frame of the tool; now you can cut the waste out. You must be sure the size of the saw frame will accommodate every turn you need to make.

7 Measure, mark and cut the nine treads H from the hardboard, cut the slots which locate them on the stair strings, and do a dry fitting with the dowels as well. When you are satisfied they are perfectly square, disassemble and glue all the dowels and treads, then assemble it all. Drill 1.5mm/¹⁄₃₂in holes through the back under edge of the string into the dowels, and knock 12mm/½in panel pins into the dowels to hold everything up tight. You might need to adjust the slots and the fit of the stairs when you insert them into floor and walls, but this can be done with the stairs assembled.

8 Cut the three pieces for the fireplace, round off the corners of the mantel shelf with the coping saw and glasspaper, and drill, glue and screw-fix them together. Then cut a piece of black self-adhesive surfacing paper ('Fablon') the size of the chimney piece, but don't stick it on until the wall has been painted.

Drill one hole through from the outside of the right-hand outer wall B for a no. 6 × 12mm/½in screw, bradawl through that into the back of one of the fireplace verticals and screw up, then drill through to the other vertical and screw that too.

9 Unscrew the pillars and crosspieces in the main structure, then slot the internal walls N and O into the upper floor D and slide it into position in the slots in the walls and back, inserting the staircase at the same time. This is where you have to have five hands! You will almost certainly find that slots, notches, tongues and the general fit need adjustment, but do it patiently with small cuts of the chisel, block plane or coping saw, taking your time over this part.

When everything sits nicely, screw the

pillars and crosspieces back. Cut the upper floor ceiling E and its central upper batten; drill, screw and fix them together with no. 6 × 12mm/½in screws, and lay it over the top of the inner and outer walls with the batten resting on the tops of the outer walls B.

THE ROOF

10 Mark and cut the blanks and then the shapes for the roof gable ends G. Cut the battens by mitring one end of the pieces, then laying them overlength on the angled edges of the gable. Draw a vertical line from base to apex of the gable, then with the mitred end of the batten at the top, slide it down so you leave a 2mm/³⁄₃₂in gap from the line to the parallel cut end of the batten. Then mark along the bottom edge of the gable across the batten to get the angle and length exactly right for the 4mm/³⁄₁₆in gap you need to leave for the ridge tile piece P.

Drill, glue and screw the battens with the 3mm/⁷⁄₆₄in drill through the gable, bradawling into the batten, and using the no. 6 × 12mm/½in screws.

11 Now draw up a full size grid for the bargeboards, draw out their full shape then transfer that via a tracing to the 25 × 13mm/1 × ½in softwood pieces. Note they are different sizes at each end, because of the chimney. Drill through

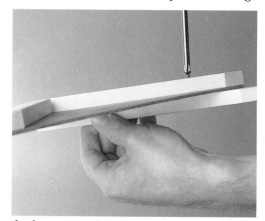

the battens and gables with the 5mm/³⁄₁₆in drill and screw the bargeboards on, coming from inside with no. 8 × 25mm/1in screws.

12 Cut the 25 × 25mm/1 × 1in softwood for the ridge post, carve the bottom finial decoration, drill a 6.5mm/¼in hole centrally in the other end, and drill the same size hole through the middle of the 20mm/¾in wooden ball.

Push a hole with the bradawl into the ball before you try to drill it, because the drill can slip. Now cut a 35mm/1⅜in length of 6.5mm dowel, and drill another hole in the centre of another piece of 25 × 25mm/1 × 1in scrap; cut it about 20mm/¾in long and shape it how you want for the top – conical or what you will – then slip the dowel into the bottom post, slip the ball over the dowel, and slot the top piece on. If it all looks OK, take them apart and glue them; if they need more work, adjust size and shape (or start again!) until you're satisfied, then glue them together and drill and screw the ridge post on to the left-hand gable end (as you face the house) with 5mm/³⁄₁₆in drill and no. 8 × 25mm/1in screws.

13 Measure, mark and cut the blank for the ridge-tile piece P from the 4mm/³⁄₁₆in ply and cut the shapes to resemble the tiles along the top. Make sure you get the marking out right, or the tiles will end up different sizes. Tidy up the curves with the half-round fine-cut file or a piece of glasspaper wrapped round a bit of dowel. Cut the three triangular ridge supports from the 25 × 13mm/1 × ½in softwood and cut the 4mm/³⁄₁₆in slots in their tops for the ridge P to sit in; glue them on in the positions shown on the drawing.

14 Cut out the two roof pieces F from the hardboard and drill them with the 3mm/⅛in drill; countersink the holes. Remember at this stage you will be screwing through into the battens on the gables, which already have some screws in them; work out the positions so the screws won't foul. Chamfer the angle on the top edges of the roof pieces with the block plane to come up against the ridge-tile piece without a gap. Hold everything together while you bradawl or pilot drill (2mm/³⁄₃₂in), if you need to, into the battens on the gables and the ridge supports.

The glue on the latter should be dry before you do this. Screw a few screws in to hold it all reasonably tight then test fit it over the main structure; the battens and edges of the gables G should sit comfortably on the top edges of the outer walls. If everything fits, screw the whole assembly up tight with no. 6 × 12mm/½in screws.

THE CHIMNEY

15 Mark and cut the four chimney sides I full size, and the four chimney battens. Drill (3mm/⅛in) and countersink to glue and screw the front and back chimney faces over the edges of the two side ones with the no. 6 × 12mm/½in screws. The box formed thus becomes 70 × 76mm/2¾ × 3in. The battens should

be set down inside 3mm/⅛in to hold the top piece J.

Trim the box square at the bottom, then set a 45° angle on your bevel gauge and mark from the bottom corners of one of the 76mm/3in sides to where the marks meet, forming a 90° vee. Cut along those lines, through to the other face, and test the fit over the roof; you have cut through the battens as well, which means the screws you have used must not be in the way of the saw! When the fit is good, cut the brick ridge pieces X and mitre them round the chimney; fitting and marking as you go; just glue will hold them well enough.

Cut the top piece J and drill a 12mm/½in hole in the centre, then cut the 38mm/1½in dowel for the chimney itself, mark it and carve it to shape. Drill a 12mm/½in hole in the centre of the bottom, glue a piece of 12mm/½in dowel in the bottom, and glue that in to the hole. It must not be too long to foul the piece of 25 × 13mm/1 × ½in softwood that goes across the bottom of the chimney (glue and screw it), into which a no. 8 × 50mm/2in screw will pass.

Cut and drill another triangular piece, like the roof-ridge support pieces and for the screw to pass through, through the apex of the roof; bradawl or pilot (3mm/⅛in drill) a hole through the screw hole in this piece into the bottom batten in the chimney where the screw will locate. Glue the top piece and chimney pot into the chimney.

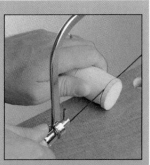

HINT
To carve a curved shape on a round piece like the chimney, hold a fine-toothed saw on the mark where the maximum depth of cut will be and turn the dowel in your fingers between the saw-blade and the bench, letting it cut as deep as you are going to go. Now you

can pare, as if you were sharpening a pencil, in cuts going deeper towards that saw-cut. Use sandpaper and a fine wood rasp to get the final smooth shape.

Outside it's an olde worlde cottage, but inside it can be furnished with every modern convenience . . .

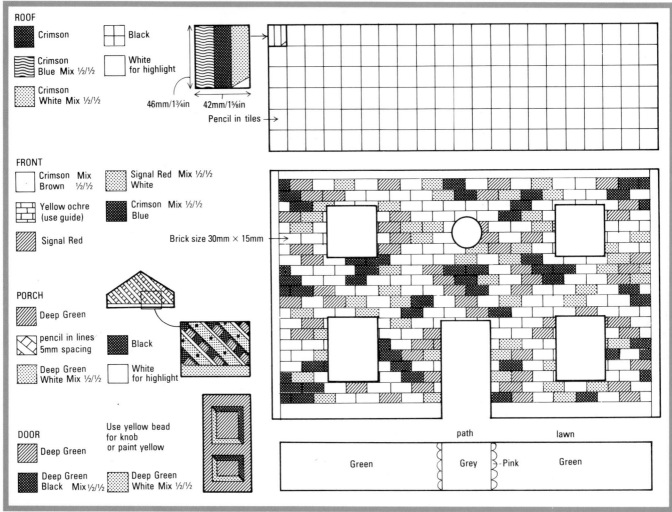

ROOF

Crimson

Black

Crimson Blue Mix ½/½

White for highlight

Crimson White Mix ½/½

46mm/1¾in   42mm/1⅝in

Pencil in tiles →

FRONT

Crimson Mix Brown ½/½

Signal Red Mix ½/½ White

Yellow ochre (use guide)

Crimson Mix ½/½ Blue

Signal Red

Brick size 30mm × 15mm →

PORCH

Deep Green

pencil in lines 5mm spacing

Black

Deep Green White Mix ½/½

White for highlight

DOOR

Deep Green

Use yellow bead for knob or paint yellow

Deep Green Black Mix ½/½

Deep Green White Mix ½/½

path   lawn

Green   Grey   Pink   Green

THE FRONT

16 Measure, mark and cut the front, M with all its window and door cut-outs, and cut the battens. Drill, glue and screw them with the 3mm/⅛in drill and the no. 6 × 12mm/½in screws. Hold it up to the open front of the house and carefully mark off the hinge recesses on the batten from the ones on the pillar, then cut them out. Fit the hinges with the no. 4 × 12mm/½in brass screws, and make sure the front swings nicely. Cut little 'turn buttons' from the ply, 20 × 10mm/¾ × ⅜in and drill a 5mm/³⁄₁₆ in hole one end so they pivot on a screw in the right-hand pillar and hold the front closed.

17 Measure, mark and cut all the window surrounds S, T and U, and test them to fit; you will be gluing them on with epoxy resin after everything is painted. Cut a sliver of 4mm/³⁄₁₆in ply, about 20 × 10mm/¾ × ⅜in, and glue it to the edge of the 'door hole' inside the front for the catch; then drill a 3mm/⅛in hole in the door, enlarge the hole in the yellow bead to take the 3mm/⅛in bolt head (the 5mm/³⁄₁₆in bit should do it), slip the bolt into the bead and fill it with car body filler.

Cut the 25 × 25mm/1 × 1in square of 22g brass in half with the fine hacksaw and drill 3mm/⅛in holes in the end of each piece; then slip the bolt through the hole in the door and a nut, washer, brass strip, washer and nut over the bolt and tighten up. Screw the other brass strip to the ply piece you have glued on the inside of the front with a no. 6 × 6mm/¼in self-tapping screw, bending it out slightly so the catch on the door will sit into it. Position the piece on the door frame by 'hanging' the door on its carpet tape and judging where the latch comes.

18 Draw up full-size grids for the porch gables L and bargeboards V from hardboard and ply respectively, measure, mark them out with a tracing, and cut them. Cut the inner supports and brackets from softwood; for the bargeboards and the brackets you will get the width by gluing pieces of the 25 × 12mm/1 × ½in softwood edge to edge.

Cut the porch roof pieces K from hardboard, and draw a grid and trace the shape of the ridge post W; cut that out. Drill and screw the gables to the inner pieces, and

the inner pieces through to the brackets with no. 6 × 12mm/½in and no. 8 × 25mm/1in screws respectively, but don't fix the bargeboards and ridge post yet because they must be painted first. Just test them for fit at this stage. Cut the nameboard Y and drill it and the gable for the .5mm/¹⁄₆₄in brass wire with the 1.5mm/¹⁄₁₆in drill.

PAINTING

19 Disassemble everything you can, clean it all up with medium then fine glasspaper, and prime every surface with white emulsion (water-based latex US) to seal it. Follow the colours carefully, mixing where you have to, using either non-toxic modelling enamels over two coats of varnish, or acrylics which you must then cover with varnish for protection. Draw floorboard lines on to the floors with the permanent black marker, making sure the lines are straight and evenly spaced, and varnish over them to fix them.

WINDOWS

20 When everything is dry, reassemble it all, gluing (epoxy resin glue over paint) and screwing the porch on – from the inside. Cut the perspex windows with a hacksaw and fit them in the holes; cover them with white adhesive 'washable surface' ('Fablon'), and mark and cut out

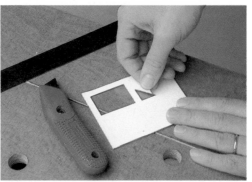

the window 'frames' with a craft knife, peeling off the waste pieces. Set the windows into the holes, retaining them with 'Fablon' from the inside, then glue the window surrounds S, T and U on to the front with epoxy resin glue.

Hang the door with carpet tape, write the name of the house with black marker on the name-board Y and hang it with the .5mm/¹⁄₆₄in brass wire.

PUFFING BILLY

In these days of super-sleek 125mph passenger trains and highly sophisticated electronic toys, it is still the age of steam that fires the imagination. When the old lady said 'If God had meant us to fly He would never have given us the railways', she wasn't talking about diesel locomotives, Inter City or Amtrak, which is why this classic puffer, complete with smoke, will be every bit as popular with children (adults too!) as Thomas the Tank Engine and his friends in the station yard. We show you how to make the carriage in the picture, but there is no need to stop at one. Why not make a whole string of carriages to the same design, paint them different colours, and add them to the train.

There is really nothing complicated about the construction; accurate drilling of the chassis sides for the wheels is important, so the axles will line up properly across the body. Once you have made one carriage, why not make a few more – some goods trucks, perhaps, a Pullman carriage or two, or a guard's van? The colour scheme is also a matter of choice, as are the moving 'Goo-goo' eyes; you can buy these from hobby shops in various designs and sizes, or make your own; or add personal touches for the crew, like the child's name on the front. The engine itself, of course, should definitely have a name of its own.

BODY COMPONENTS

1 Measure, mark and cut out all the pieces for the main panels of the bodies from the 9mm/⅜in ply, either by straight measuring or from a full-size gridded drawing. These are pieces A–H; coach and engine roofs, the two bases, the coach and engine sides, the four chassis sides, the smoke and the three body ends.

The smoke will need the grid treatment, unless you want to trust to your own artistic talent!

Place one of the bases over the carriage roof A, position it centrally, and drill a 6.5mm/¼in hole in each corner as shown right through the base and into the underside of the roof to total depth of 15mm/⅝in.

Drill out the old-fashioned round windows

MATERIALS

Plywood exact sizes; softwood lengths exact, widths and thicknesses nominal

Birch faced plywood	Metric			Imperial		
A Coach roof	1	178mm×	89mm×9mm	7in×	3½in	×⅜in
B Engine roof	1	89 ×	89 ×9	3½	×3½	×⅜
C Base	2	172 ×	64 ×9	6¾	×2½	×⅜
D Coach side	2	108 ×	82 ×9	4¼	×3¼	×⅜
E Engine cab side	2	70 ×	82 ×9	2¾	×3¼	×⅜
F Chassis side	4	172 ×	38 ×9	6¾	×1½	×⅜
G Smoke	1	108 ×	45 ×9	4¼	×1¾	×⅜
H Body ends	3	70 ×	64 ×9	2¾	×2½	×⅜
Banister rail						
J Boiler	1	75 ×	50 ×50	3	× 2	×2
First quality (FAS) softwood (pine)						
I Firebox	1	57 ×	50 ×25	2¼	× 2	×1
Hardwood strip						
K Chassis ends/ boiler support	5	64 ×	12 ×3	2½	× ½	×⅛
Hardwood dowel						
L Coach roof supports	4	92 ×	6.5 dia.	3⅝	× ¼ dia.	
M Axles	4	64 ×	6.5 dia.	2½	× ¼ dia.	
N Fixings	10	12 ×	6.5 dia.	½	× ¼ dia.	
O Dome	1	25 ×	12 dia.	1	× ½ dia.	
P Buffers	8	12 ×	12 dia.	½	× ½ dia.	
Q Chimney	1	42 ×	18 dia.	1⅝	× ¾ dia.	
Wheels	8		50 dia.		2 dia.	

Screw hook and eye
Eyes 8–10mm 'Goo-goo' or make them yourself
Glasspaper medium, fine
Non-toxic acrylic or modelling enamel paints
Wood glue and epoxy resin glue

TOOLS

Pencil, tracing paper, card, carbon
  paper
Bradawl
Try square
Tenon saw
Coping or jigsaw
Hand or electric drill
Bits: 7mm/⁹⁄₃₂, 6.5mm/¼in,
12mm/½in, 18mm/¾in flat bit
Block plane or Surform shaper
  plane
G-cramps
Steel rule, flexible rule
25mm/1in paintbrush, fine artist's
  brush

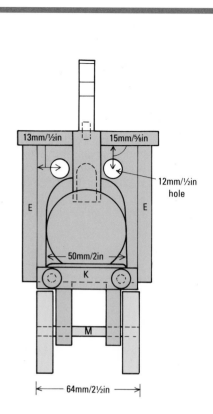

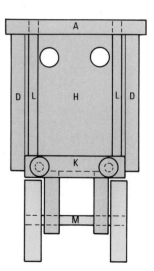

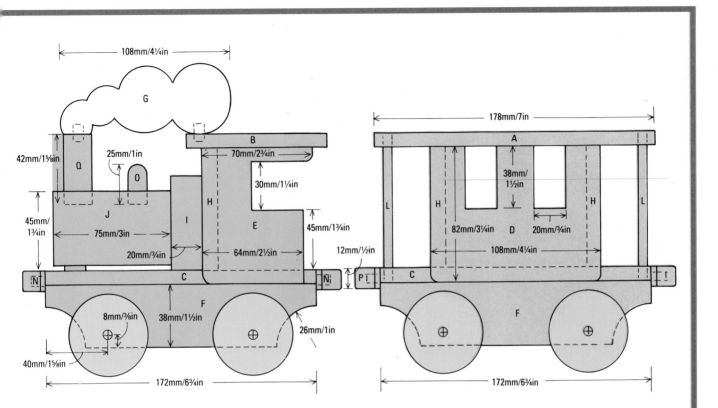

108mm/4¼in

G

42mm/1⅝in

Q

25mm/1in

O

B

70mm/2¾in

30mm/1¼in

H

J

I

E

45mm/1¾in

75mm/3in

20mm/¾in

64mm/2½in

45mm/1¾in

N

C

N

F

8mm/⅜in

38mm/1½in

26mm/1in

40mm/1⅝in

172mm/6¾in

178mm/7in

A

38mm/1½in

L

H

H

L

82mm/3¼in

D

20mm/¾in

12mm/½in

P

C

108mm/4¼in

I

F

172mm/6¾in

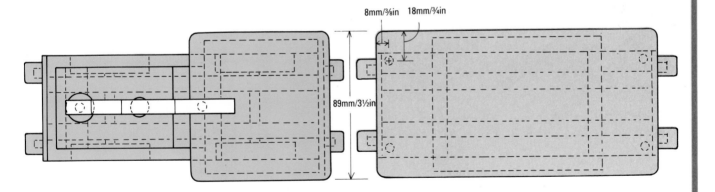

8mm/⅜in   18mm/¾in

89mm/3½in

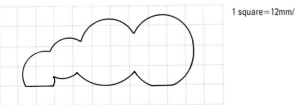

1 square = 12mm/½in

in the coach and engine ends H with the 12mm/½in bit.

Cut the curves for the chassis sides F – again using a full-size grid for marking out – and drill the axle holes in the positions shown with the 7mm/⁹⁄₃₂in bit. This is best

done by cutting them near the line, then holding all four together in the vice to give them exactly the same shape, and drilling while they are all together too. Square lines across the undersides of the bases C to position the chassis sides accurately, and glue them to the bases 12mm/½in in from the edges.

2 Cut and shape the firebox I from the drawing and the boiler J to length; drill the 18mm/¾in hole for the chimney and the 12mm/½in hole for the dome in the positions shown, both 6.5mm/¼in deep. If you are using eyes with pegs already fixed, drill the holes for them at this stage.

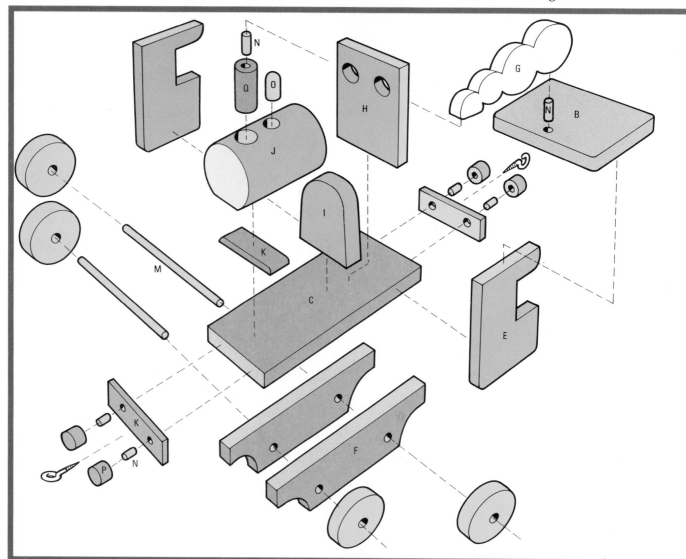

3 Make the cut-outs for the coach sides D and engine sides E using the technique described for windows in the zoo truck, and glue the coach sides to two ends H and the engine sides to the remaining one. Put the roof pieces down flat and glue the sides standing up, so the flat surface will give you a proper line.

Cut the five chassis ends/boiler supports K to length from the hardwood strip, and mark and drill 6.5mm/¼in holes for the buffers in four of them as shown. Put the assembled engine cab on the base C you have not drilled, and glue the firebox to the cab; put the other piece K on the base

25mm/1in from the front, and glue the boiler to it and to the firebox at the other end. Don't get glue onto the base. You must separate the boiler/cab from the base for painting. Glue the four chassis ends K that you have drilled on to the ends of each base, flush with the top.

4 Cut the funnel Q from the 18mm/ ¾in dowel and drill the centre with a 6.5mm/¼in hole, 6.5mm/ ¼in deep. Cut the dome O from the 12mm/ ½in dowel and sand it to shape; glue both pieces into the boiler, remembering to keep the chimney hole up! Cut all 10 6.5mm/¼in dowel fixings N and glue one into the top of the chimney.

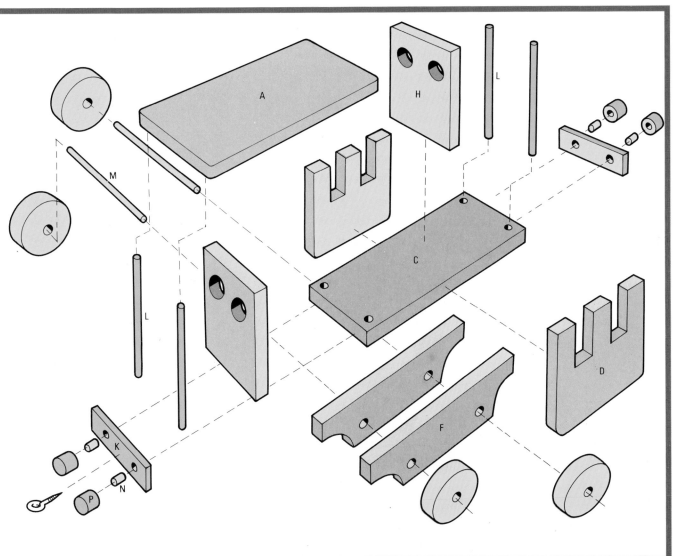

Drill two 6.5mm/¼in holes in the smoke as shown; lay the engine roof B in position on the cab, and dry fit the smoke on the chimney so it

comes on to the cab; mark the place where you'll need to drill for the other smoke fixing dowel. Take the roof off and drill the 6.5mm/¼in hole 6.5mm/¼in deep. Cut the

eight buffers P from 12mm/½in dowel, and centre drill them all 6.5mm/¼in deep with the 6.5mm/¼in drill. Glue the dowel fixings N into those holes, then glue the other ends into the drilled chassis end pieces K.

Cut the four roof supports L to length from the 6.5mm/¼in dowel, and the axles M from the same thickness of dowel; the axle lengths are crucial, so pay special attention here. Drill the wheels in their centres 6.5mm/¼in to a depth of 6.5mm/¼in.

6 Dry assemble the whole thing, adjusting axle lengths and roof support dowels if necessary, and generally making sure everything fits good and square.

Take it all apart again and sand everything thoroughly, paying special attention to the inside edges of the windows, and then paint it in the colours you want, either with acrylic paints and varnish over the top, or varnish as a base for modelling enamels. Mask off the areas of different

HINT
If you make a dowel hole in the wrong place or it is otherwise a mistake, you can just glue a piece of dowel into it and trim it off flush. Sand it and it will be difficult to know the difference.

colours and allow them to dry thoroughly before you do the next ones. If you are going to use 'ordinary' wood glue, you must mask off gluing areas too.

7 Now you can glue everything together; the engine is easy, with the cab just going down on the base. The carriage supports must all be of equal height; gently tap the roof to get it flat, and you might have to trim a bit of dowel underneath if it is still too long.

Drop glue into one wheel, put the axle in it, pass it through the chassis sides, and glue the other wheel on; repeat for all the wheels.

Finally mark the position of the screw hooks and eyes for the coach and engine in between the buffers, and screw the hook into the engine and the eye into the coach. If you have another screw eye, fix that in the front of the engine and you can tie string to it for a pull-along.

HINT
An ordinary 'twist bit' is often not good enough for drilling for dowel joints – especially where there is a shallow 'blind hole' – because the shoulders of the drill are quite steep. You can get drill bits with sharp 'wings' and a centre point which cuts a hole with much cleaner edges.

ROCK-A-BYE BABY

An essential piece of equipment for every baby doll owner, the doll's cradle will be the focus of countless games of mothers and fathers – and there's many an adult father who loves to put his own children to bed, so why not encourage your sons to have the fun too? This charming design is distinctly 'cottagey', with its country-style curved hood frame, grille and decorative wooden balls. Made throughout in first quality softwood (pine), it will be a lasting joy for more than one generation of children.

As with most toy designs, the components are comparatively easy to cut and fit, but there are a lot of slats. Cutting many pieces all the same length is easily done with a simple cutting jig like the one described in the instructions for the zoo truck. You can paint the crib a pastel shade if you like, or add small patterns with stencils to decorate the woodwork.

MATERIALS

Lengths exact, widths and thicknesses nominal

First quality (FAS) PAR softwood (pine).

		Metric			Imperial		
A Ends	2	280mm	×175mm	×15mm	11in	×6½in	×⅝in
B Spine frame	1	556	×175	×15	21⅞	×6½	×⅝
C Rockers	2	404	×175	×15	16	×6½	×⅝
D Side slats	10	392	× 25	×9	15⅜	×1	×⅜
E Canopy front	2	255	× 67	×15	10	×2⅝	×⅝
F Canopy back	2	192	×141	×15	7 9/16	×5½	×⅝
G Canopy slats	17	182	× 25	×9	7¼	×1	×⅜
H Grille	6	90	× 15	×9	3½	× ⅝	×⅜
I Front strengthener	1	60	× 15	×9	2⅜	× ⅝	×⅜
J Floor slats	7	354	× 25	×9	13⅞	×1	×⅜
K Central floor supports	2	238	× 25	×15	9⅜	× 1	×⅝
L End floor supports	4	112	× 15	×15	4⅜	× ⅝	×⅝
M Lug	1	40	× 40	×9	1⅝	×1⅝	×⅜
N Lugs	2	30	× 30	×9	1⅛	×1⅛	×⅜
O Balls	2	36 dia			1⅜ dia.		
Hardwood dowel							
Fixings		600	× 6.5 dia.		24	× ¼ dia.	
Screws: Twinfast countersunk	30	no. 6×15			no. 6×⅝		
Panel pins:		20	×		¾	×	
		16	×		⅝	×	
Brass gimp pins (optional fixings)		20	×		¾	×	
		16	×		⅝	×	

Medium and fine glasspaper, non-toxic polyurethane varnish, wood glue (PVA) and/or epoxy resin glue.

IMPORTANT NOTE

The constant difficulty about specifying sizes for softwood that is planed before you buy it arises here; 'nominal' widths and thicknesses are stated in the cutting list, but your bought timber will undoubtedly be narrower and thinner than nominal. The drawings therefore show the slots and notches where pieces fit into each other at the sizes in which PAR (planed all round) softwood usually comes. 25 × 9mm/1 × ⅜in, for instance, has been shown as finishing to 22 × 6mm/⅞ × ¼in. Likewise the wide board from which you will take the main components should be bought as 175 × 15mm/7 × ⅝in, but it will be nearer 168 × 12mm/6 ⅝ × ½in in fact. Be sure to measure every dimension carefully before you do any cutting, and revise the dimensions shown on the drawings of the slots and notches if this is necessary. Take your time preparing and you can't go wrong.

TOOLS

Pencil, paper, tracing paper, carbon paper
Steel rule, flexible rule
Try square
Bevel gauge
G-cramps
Electric jigsaw and/or coping or fretsaw
Tenon saw
Bradawl
Pin hammer
Screwdriver
Chisels: 6mm/¼in, 12mm/½in, 19mm/¾in
Pincers
Electric or hand drill
Pliers
Drill bits: 1mm/3/64in, 2mm/3/32in, 3mm/⅛in, 6.5mm/¼ in, 10mm/⅜in,
Block plane
Fine wood rasps and files
Marking knife or craft knife
25mm/1in flat brush
12mm/½in flat brush

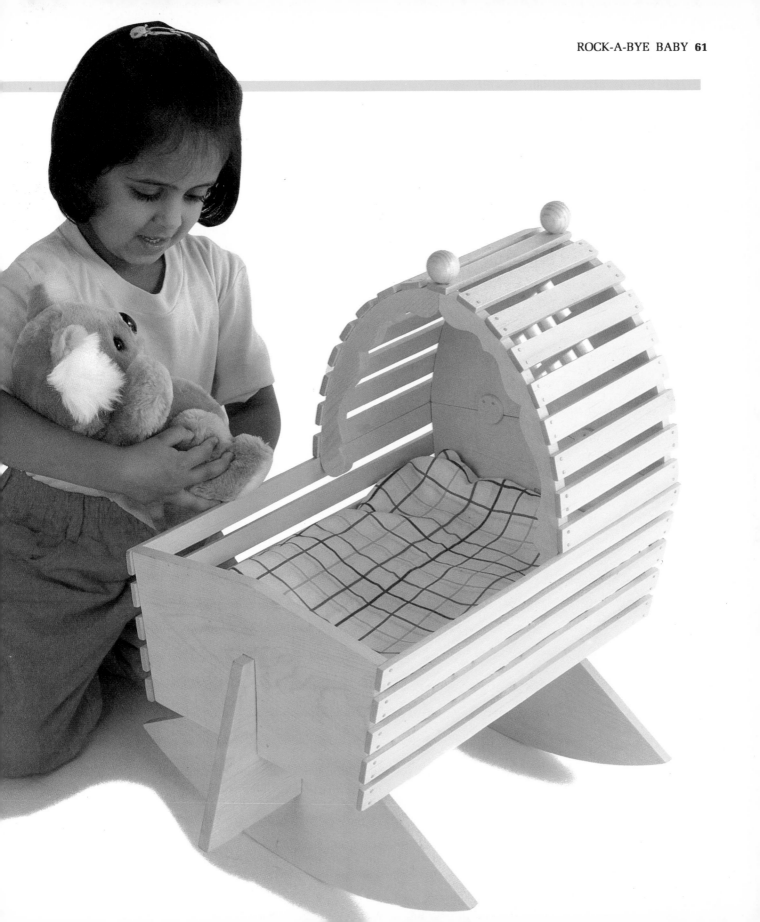

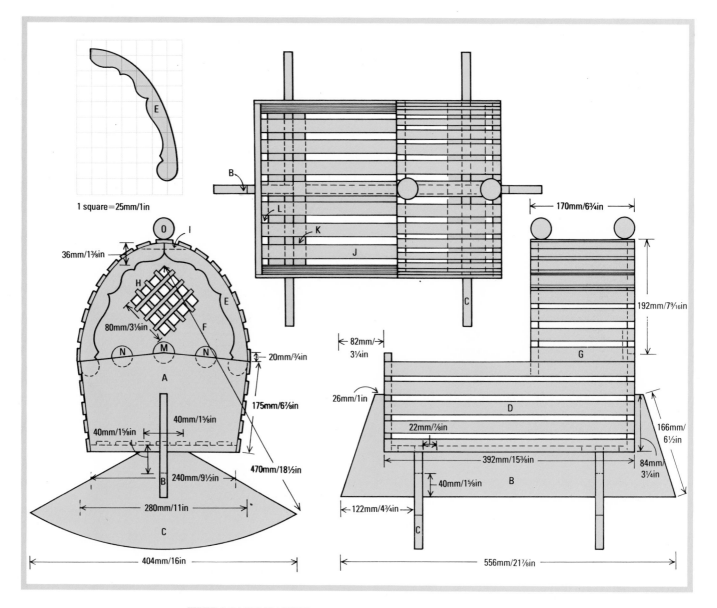

1 square = 25mm/1in

THE MAIN PARTS

1 When you have bought the wood, check the widths and thicknesses, look the drawings over, and decide whether you need to alter any of the dimensions of the slots where the components fit together.

Measure and mark out the components on the wide board, either by straightforward measuring or by drawing up a full-size grid on the board itself and tracing the shapes of the components on to that. For the straight-sided pieces which nevertheless have angles, such as the ends A, you can use the bevel gauge.

Cut all the straight lines with the tenon saw and the inside corners and more complex curved shapes with the jigsaw or coping saw. Cut out all the slots where the parts fit, testing them with their relevant parts and trimming them with the 19mm/¾in chisel if need be; also cut out the shaped canopy front pieces E, and the 'half-holes' in the two canopy back pieces F. Don't notch them for the grille yet.

2 Cut the grille pieces H to rough length (about 9mm/⅜in over), and clamp them all together on edge on the bench with G-cramps. Now square off right across all six at both ends, measuring the exact length carefully; cut them to length. Then mark out the positions of the notches on the edges, right across all six, still cramped together, and the depth of the notches – the wood will probably finish to 12mm/½in, so the notches will be half that or 6mm/¼in – on the outside faces of the

two outside pieces. Carefully cut with the tenon saw just on the inside of the notch lines down to the depth lines, then come in from either side with the 6mm/¼in chisel, removing the waste.

THE CANOPY ENDS

4 Cramp or wedge the two halves of the canopy back F together flat on the bench, fit the grille pieces into each other, and lay the assembled grille over the hole, lining it up so the ends of the grille pieces overlap the wood of the canopy back 5mm/³⁄₁₆in all round. Mark and cut out the notches for the grille, then using the same cramping system with

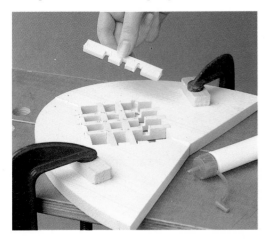

which you have held them, glue the two halves together, and glue the grille in place.

3 Set the two halves of the canopy front E up together vertically in the vice, their meeting surfaces hard together at the top middle as if they were already joined. They should just protrude above the top of the vice jaws. Take a short piece of the 15 × 9mm/⅝ × ⅜in soft-wood for the strengthener I and hold it in position across the join centrally along the thickness of the canopy front pieces; mark

either side. Then carefully cut a slot across the top curve formed by both pieces, about 12mm/½in deep at the maximum, and carefully chisel it out with the 6mm/¼in chisel. Test fit the strengthener piece I all the time, for the fit here must be tight but not so tight that you force the sides of the slot apart.

Loosen the vice, take the two halves apart slightly and glue the meeting surfaces; place them hard together again, drop some more glue in the slot, and push the oversize strengthener piece I into the slot. Leave it in the vice while the glue dries, and when it is set hard lay the whole shape over the canopy back and put them together in the vice. Trim the strengthener

down to the curve, then block-plane, rasp and sand the two components together in the vice so the shapes are exactly the same.

5 Cut to length and drill with the 3mm/⁷⁄₆₄in drill four holes in the end floor supports L. Place them along each side of the bottom inside edges of the ends A and drill through into the ends with the 2mm/³⁄₃₂in drill; glue and screw them to the ends. Then slip the ends over the high ends of the spine frame B so that the inside faces of the ends A are flush with the vertical endgrain of the cutout in the spine frame.

The top edges of the floor supports L should be flush with the long edge of the bottom of the cutout.

SLATS

6 Cut all the side slats D to about 3mm/¹⁄₈in overlength, using a cutting jig of the kind described in the zoo truck chapter. Test nail with a 16mm ⁵⁄₈in panel pin through the end of a piece of

scrap, and see if the wood splits; if it does, you will have to drill holes for the temporary fixing panel pins in the end of each one. Try snipping the ends off the panel

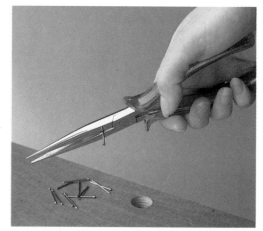

pins with pliers, so you are pushing a blunt end through the wood fibres, instead of trying to part them with a sharp end; it might work. The photo shows the slats

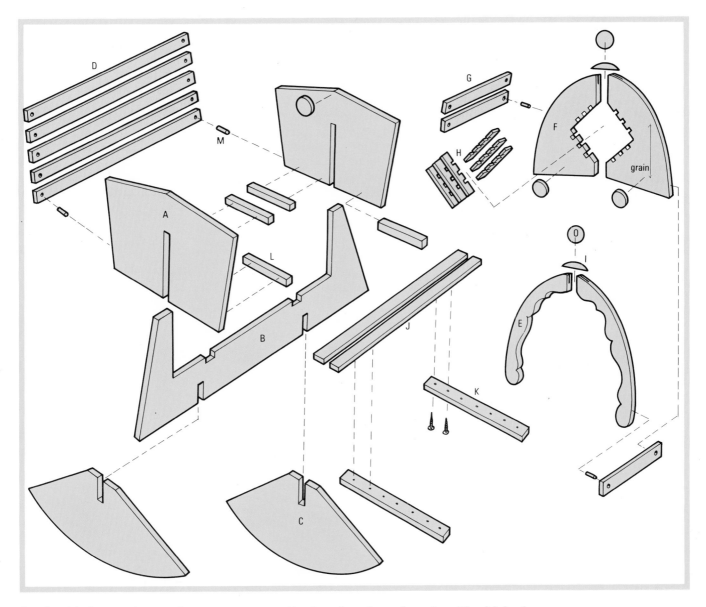

fixed with brass pins, and you can use these if you wish – in which case you will have to drill two holes in each end of each slat with the 1mm/³⁄₆₄in drill. A laborious task. For safety reasons it is generally good practice to avoid the use of nails in toys wherever possible, so use the temporary panel pin fixing plus dowels if you can.

Glue and pin the slats on the edges of the ends, spacing them equally; don't tap the pins all the way in, but leave about 6mm/¼in protruding. When the glue is dry, pull the panel pins out with the pincers, drill 6.5mm/¼in holes straight through the slats into the ends, cut short lengths of 6.5mm/

¼in dowel, and tap them in with a blob of glue.

Leave the ends just proud and trim them with chisel and block plane when the glue is dry. As you fix the slats, try and get one set of ends perfectly lined up; it is a good idea to do this against a piece of board held vertically in the vice or on the bench with cramps, so you can push the end of each new slat you fix up to that. When the glue and dowels are dry, square lines fractionally in from the slightly uneven ends of the slats, and carefully trim with the block plane and chisel to the lines. Be extra careful not to break off little pieces of endgrain.

7 Cut all the canopy slats G and fix them in the same way as the side slats, noting that the ends of the front E are lower than the outside edges of the back F; the best way is to hold the front E upright in the vice – put two long battens across the bottom 'legs' if the vice jaws are not wide enough – and adjust the height by holding the back F upright on the bench right next to the front in the vice. Line up the tops of the two parts. Then you can set the back F away on the bench the right distance for the slats, and fix them all.

Drill two 6.5mm/¼in holes in the top centre of the canopy front and back, and drill the two wooden balls with the same size holes.

Cut two short lengths of 6.5mm/¼in dowel and glue them into the balls and then into the holes in the tops of the canopy.

Cut out the locating lugs M and N and glue them in position on the inside bottom edges of the canopy back F and the back crib end A. Glue the rockers C into their slots in the spine frame B.

FLOOR

9 Cut all the floor slats J precisely to length on the cutting jig, if you are using one; or cut one exactly to length then mark all the other pieces out from that 'master'. Cut the central floor supports K, and carefully mark the centre of their width down the endgrain at each end of both. Measure precisely from centre to centre of the notches in the spine frame in which the supports sit, then nail very lightly the two support slats to the bench – get them parallel to each other by squaring them off the edge of the bench – with the centre marks exactly as far apart as the centres of the notches. The tips of the panel pins should just go into the surface of the bench – just enough to stop the pieces moving – and the pins should be placed towards the ends, in positions where they will not be covered by the slats.

Lay two slats over the supports with their ends exactly the same distance from the centres of the supports as they will be when inside the crib. Square a higher and dead straight piece of wood up to the two ends of the two slats, and carefully pin them to the supports, checking measurements as you go and leaving most of the pin protruding. Cramp that larger piece square on, then all you have to do is 'half pin' all the other slats in place, bringing them up to the large locating piece.

Now very carefully lift the whole assembly off the bench so the supports come away from the bench but not the slats from the supports, and turn the whole thing upside down; rest it on two thick pieces of wood which are higher than the protruding length of the panel pins so the pins don't come into contact with the bench. The thick pieces should be just close to the supports. Drill the supports with the 3mm/⅛in drill, taking care not to go into the slats, and screw them with the no. 6 × 15mm/⅝in screws. Turn it all over and remove all the pins. Test for fit in the crib, and trim a little if you need to. There may be some movement, but it will be fine once it is sitting in the crib.

10 Sand the whole thing carefully with medium then fine glasspaper, then varnish it with three coats of the polyurethane varnish, rubbing down lightly between coats.

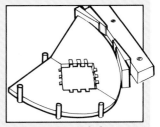

LITTLE RED RACER

This old style racing car has a touch of vintage elegance, recalling the days of Brooklands and Le Mans. It could be any one of the many stylish racing cars which abounded in the 1930s, but whatever the imagination makes it 'on the road', it's quite simple to make, consisting basically of two pieces of wood. The shaping on the bonnet and boot is clearly marked on the drawings, but with a bit of extra length in the body you can have a 'boat tail' or other distinctive classic features.

TOOLS

Pencil, paper, tracing paper, carbon
Hand or electric drill
Try square
Compass
Drill bits 6.5mm/¼in, 3.5mm/
   ⁹⁄₆₄in, 12mm/½in, 32mm/1¼in
   flat bit
Steel rule and flexible rule
Electric jigsaw or coping saw
Block plane or Surform shaper plane
Screwdriver
Small hammer
Fine half-round file
19mm/¾in chisel
G-cramps
25mm/1in brush
Fine artist's paintbrush

PIT LANE

MATERIALS

Exact lengths; nominal widths/thicknesses

First quality (FAS) softwood (pine)

		Metric			Imperial		
Base		250mm×	75mm×25mm		9⅞in×	3in×1in	
Body		235 ×	75 ×50		9¼ ×	3 ×2	

Hardwood dowel		60	× 32 dia.		2½ ×	1¼ dia.	
		12	× 6 dia.		½ ×	¼ dia.	

Wooden wheels	4		75 dia.			3 dia.	
Wooden ball	1		32 dia.			1¼ dia.	
Screws: Bright							
zinc r/head	4	no. 12 ×38			no. 12 ×1½		
Washers	4	no. 12 internal dia.					
Medium and fine glasspaper							
Wood glue							
Non-toxic acrylic or modelling enamel paints							

Like most of the wheeled toys in this book, the design uses wooden wheels bought from a hobby or toy supplier, but you can make your own. Some tips for doing this using a power drill and sanding disc are found with the instructions on how to make the Fire Engine. Many of the toys also use 'peg' people, which are easy to make if you have a wood lathe and some experience, but here's how to do it if you have no access to a lathe; get a length (about 60mm/2½in) of 25mm/1in or 32mm/1¼in dowel, a wooden ball the same diameter (from hobby shops or hardware stores), and about 32mm/1¼in of 6mm/¼in dowel. Drill a 6.5mm/¼in hole in the ball – use a centre

punch to start the drill off – and another in the centre of the dowel. Mark the centre and punch it again, as the drill will tend to wander. Put a blob of glue in the holes in the ball and big dowel, tap the small dowel into the ball and then the other end into the big dowel. When the glue is dry, trim the 'shoulders' with a sharp knife or chisel.

HINT
Most glue joints are far better when held with G-cramps while the glue dries. Be careful to pad the wood if you use cramps to stop it bruising. Glue will also hold better if you roughen the surfaces to be glued with the teeth of a saw or coarse glasspaper.

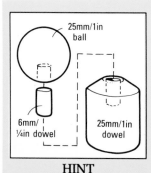

HINT
To make a simple 'peg' person take a length (about 60mm/2½in) of 25mm/1in dowel, a wooden ball the same diameter and 32mm/1in of 6mm/¼in dowel. Drill 6.5mm/¼in holes in the ball and the centre of the big dowel. Put blobs of glue in both holes. Tap one end of the small dowel into the ball, and the other into the big dowel. Wait for glue to dry, then trim 'shoulders' with a knife.

1 Mark and cut the body blank to length. Mark out and cut with a tenon saw and jig- or coping saw

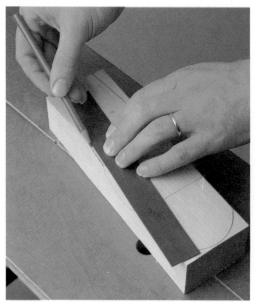

the tapering sides and rounded end.

Measure the slope on the sides, and mark the round cut-out for the 'cab' – this is best done with a pencil and compass, or use a cup or any household object of the right size to draw round. Drill the 32mm/1¼in hole for the driver in the centre before you cut the curve. Plane off the slopes and cut out the cab with the jig- or

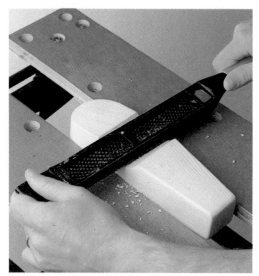

coping saw; smooth all the surfaces with medium and fine glasspaper, or in the case of the cab, the file.

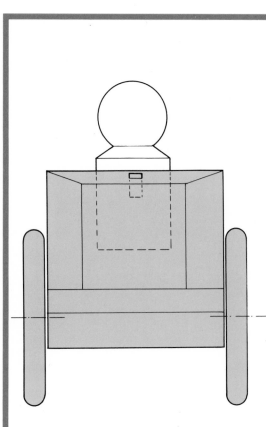

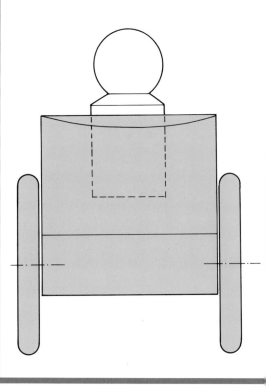

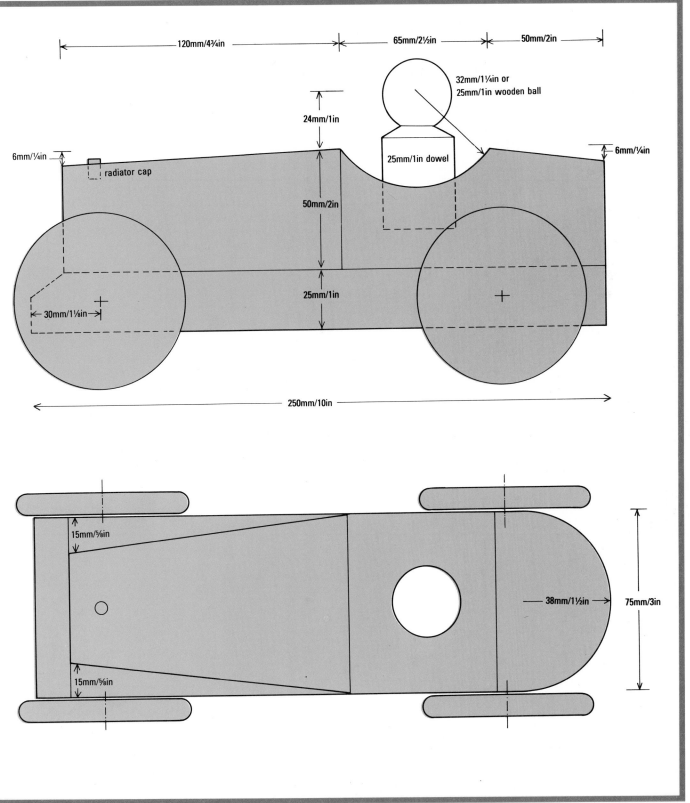

120mm/4¾in

65mm/2½in

50mm/2in

32mm/1¼in or
25mm/1in wooden ball

24mm/1in

6mm/¼in

6mm/¼in

radiator cap

25mm/1in dowel

50mm/2in

25mm/1in

30mm/1⅛in

250mm/10in

15mm/⅝in

15mm/⅝in

38mm/1½in

75mm/3in

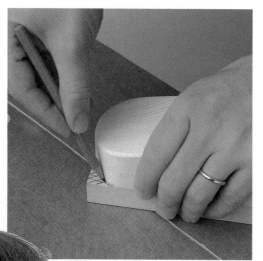

2 Cut the base to length and lay the body on to it; draw the round back on to it straight from the body, and mark at the front where the body ends. Then cut out the round on the back of the base; leave it over the line to trim when you have fixed them together.

Chamfer the slope on the front of the base with a sharp block plane or chisel.

3 Glue the top to the base. When it is dry, sand the back curve flush with the body.

Drill a 6mm/¼in hole for the radiator cap dowel, cut the dowel, put a blob of glue in the hole, and tap it in.

Cut radiator cap off to about 3mm/⅛in above the surface.

4 Make up the peg driver according to the explanation in the introduction. Fit him in the hole – he may need a bit of sanding – then put a blob of glue in the hole and tap him in.

5 Drill the centres of the wheels with the 12mm/½in flat bit deep enough to set the screw heads into – not too far! – then drill right through with the 6.5mm/¼in drill. Square faint lines across the underside of the base, and drill 3.5mm/⁹⁄₆₄in pilot holes for the screw 'axles' at exactly the same height from the bottom of the base, lined up with the line you have squared across. Note the front wheels come ahead of the base.

6 Sand everything smooth and paint all the pieces with two coats of non-toxic paint, using the colour scheme you see in the photo or your own choice of colours.

When the paint is dry mount the wheels on the screws with a washer behind, and screw them into their pilot holes; tighten them up hard then loosen them off so they'll turn nicely.

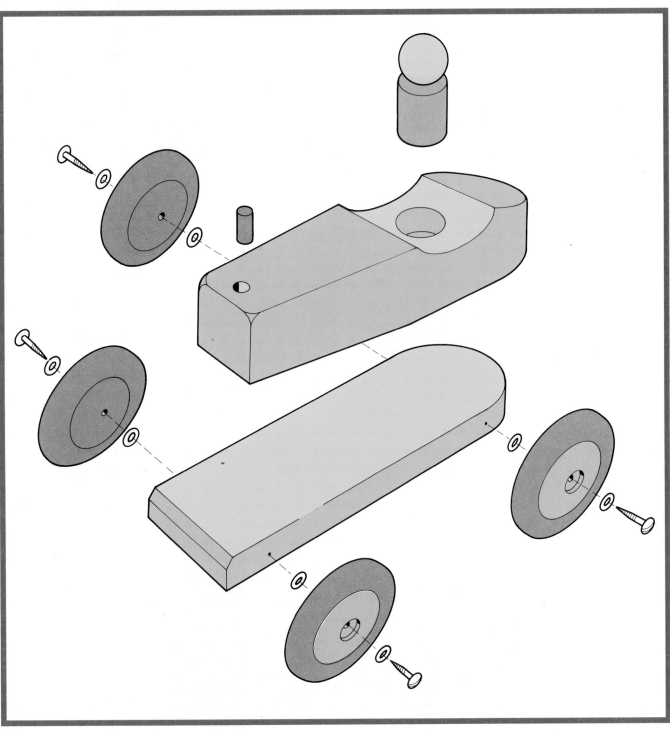

CLOWNING AROUND

The principle of toys that move or swing on a pendulum or balanced pivot is almost as old as the idea of moving toys itself – and the Egyptians had them, as did the ancient Chinese. The clowns are a trifle more modern, perhaps, but the general idea is a very old one. Which makes no difference to the endless fascination that children – and not just very young ones – will take from these jolly fellows, who somersault and swipe at each other as they go up and down and round and round on their trapeze, in parody of the popular circus act.

A simple project like this could very easily be your introduction to toymaking. The materials are really very inexpensive.

1 Draw up a full-size grid and draw out the shapes of the clowns and the 'canopy' hanger on it, then transfer them via tracing paper and carbon paper onto the 4mm/⅛in plywood. Tape the edges of the carbon and tracing paper down to stop them moving.

Cut out the two clown blanks and then their shapes, with the two blanks stuck together if you wish – for greater similarity – but you will have to use double-sided tape because the outside edges will all be cut away. Cut out the 'canopy' blank and then the shape.

2 Cut the two trapeze dowels C to length, plus the axle dowel D (12mm/½in) and the two 4mm/³⁄₁₆in pivot dowels E.

3 Drill 4mm/³⁄₁₆in holes through the clowns' hands as shown on the drawing. Clamp the two trapeze dowels C to the bench and mark the positions where the pivot-dowel E holes will go (shown on the drawing), and drill 4mm/³⁄₁₆in holes at each end but on exactly the same longitudinal axis 4mm/³⁄₁₆in deep. These holes must line up on the dowel, which is why they are clamped to the bench.

4 Clamp the 12mm/½in dowel D for the axle to the bench with some scrap wood under it and mark the positions of the two holes for the trapeze

MATERIALS

Birch faced ply		Metric			Imperial			
A Clowns	2	150mm	×150mm	×4mm	6in	× 6in	×⅛in	
B Hanger	1	150	× 40	×4	6	× 1⅝	×⅛	
Hardwood dowel								
C Trapeze	2	255	×6.5 dia.		10	× ¼ dia.		
D Axle	1	150	× 12 dia.		6	× ½ dia.		
E Pivots	2	50	× 4 dia.		2	× ³⁄₁₆ dia.		

Small screw eye, strong thread, non toxic acrylic or modelling enamel paints, non toxic polyurethane varnish, epoxy resin glue.

TOOLS

Pencil, tracing paper, carbon paper	Bits: 1.5mm/¹⁄₁₆in, 4mm/³⁄₁₆in, 6mm/¼in
Steel rule, flexible rule	Glasspaper medium and fine
Coping saw or electric jigsaw	Artist's paintbrushes
Hand or electric drill	G-cramps

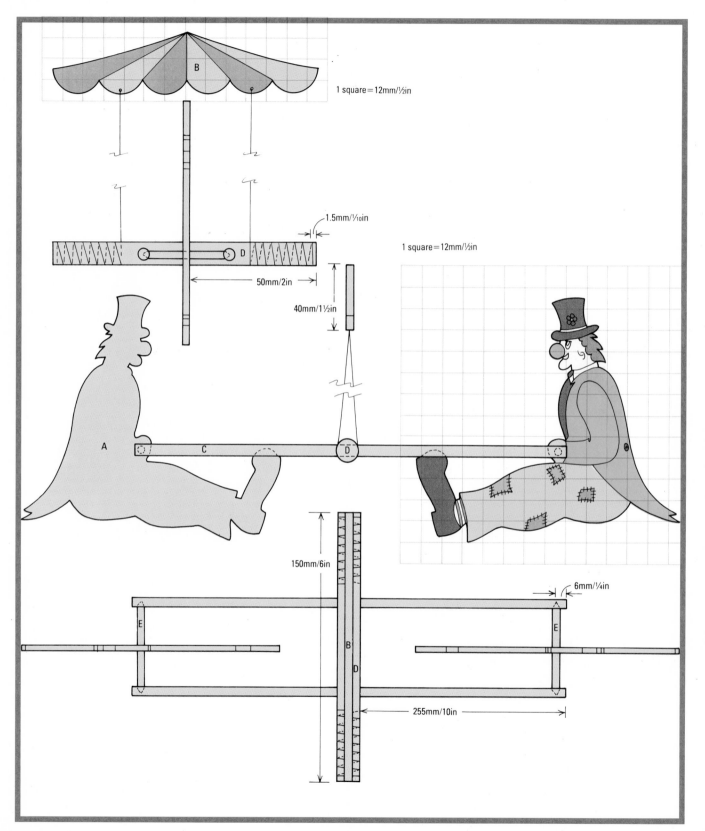

1 square = 12mm/½in

1.5mm/¹⁄₁₀in

1 square = 12mm/½in

50mm/2in

40mm/1½in

A

C

D

B

D

150mm/6in

E

6mm/¼in

E

B

D

255mm/10in

dowels C. Drill them right through with a 6.5mm/¼in drill; these holes must be perfectly vertical to both axes of the axle dowel, or there will be a warp in the finished toy and the clowns will look drunk.

5 Turn the axle dowel D through 90° on the bench and re-clamp it, then drill two 1.5mm/¹⁄₁₆in holes, one at each end, in the plane at right angles to the trapeze holes. Drill two holes the same size in the canopy hanger B where they are shown on the drawing.

6 Sand all the pieces thoroughly, then paint them, either in the colours you see in the photograph or in ones of your own choice, using non-toxic acrylics covered with two coats of non-toxic polyurethane varnish or model-

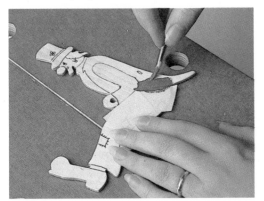

ling enamels over varnish. Mask off areas of neighbouring colour with masking tape so the colours will not bleed, and let one colour area dry before you do the one next to it. Fine detail can be drawn on with marking ink and sealed with another coat of varnish.

MOUNTING

7 Cut two lengths of the strong thread, about 600mm/24in, and knot one end of each. Pass the free end through the 1.5mm/¹⁄₁₆in holes in the axle dowel D and pull it through to the knot. Fix it there with glue. Now pass each thread through the holes you have drilled in the canopy/hanger and tie them off; screw a small eye in the top centre of the hanger and hang it somewhere convenient where you can work on it. Adjust the threads until the axle dowel D is perfectly level. Now pass each of the trapeze dowels

C through the 6.5mm/¼in holes and turn them so the pivot holes at top and bottom are facing each other.

Adjust everything until it all balances level and even; make sure the holes for the pivots E in the long trapeze dowels are perfectly on a line, and fix them in their holes in the axle with blobs of glue. Sharpen a point on the pivot dowels E with a pencil sharpener, pass them through the holes in the clowns' hands, and spring them into the holes in the long trapeze dowels C. Check to see if the clowns swing freely; if too much strain is on the trapeze dowels, shorten the pivot dowels E very slightly. Wind the clowns up on the threads, for an acrobatic display.

HINT
Rubbing down between coats of paint or varnish is not a waste of time. It gives a key for the next coat to hold well. For a super-fine finish, use 'wet and dry' silicone carbide paper when you have put your first coat on and thereafter – not on bare wood. 400-grit and 600-grit will produce an admirable finish.

BLAZE TRAILER

There's no doubt the image of the red-painted fire engine, rushing to the scene of roaring flames, is a lasting and powerful one and the focus of many a dramatic and boisterous game. Lots of shouting and, if possible, lots of water. The addition of some suitably clothed 'play people', as shown in the picture, makes the game complete, and a toy like this is bound to capture the imagination of any child.

This version of the time-honoured 'wheeled ladder' design doesn't, fortunately or unfortunately, carry water in its wooden tank, but it does have a length of hose and a winding reel to wind it out and back again. The ladder hooks on to the engine, comes off again, and stands on its old-fashioned wheels – solid and strong like most wooden toys, but with enough moving parts for a technology-tired youngster to come back to it again and again.

Though it may look quite complicated, there is nothing at all to daunt you in the making. The ladder with its row of dowel rungs just needs careful marking out; keep the long sides clamped together when you do this.

Positioning the water tank is another point to watch; you must not fix it until you have got the ladder assembly complete so you can work out where the tank should go not to foul the ladder above it.

MAKING WOODEN WHEELS

Wooden wheels are usually available from toy or hobby shops or mail-order suppliers, but if you cannot get hold of them there are ways to make their production very quick if you have a power drill.

Square up a blank and mark it across diagonally to find the centre. Set the compass and pencil to the radius you want, mark out the circle and cut it out with jig- or coping saw, cutting just outside the line.

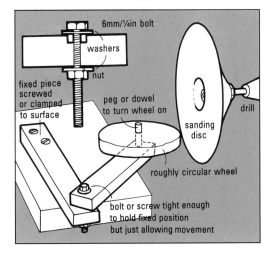

6mm/¼in bolt

washers

nut

fixed piece screwed or clamped to surface

peg or dowel to turn wheel on

drill

sanding disc

roughly circular wheel

bolt or screw tight enough to hold fixed position but just allowing movement

MATERIALS

lengths exact – widths and thicknesses nominal
First quality (FAS) softwood (pine)

		Metric			Imperial		
A Bonnet	1	60mm×	75mm×	50mm	2⅜in×	3in×	2in
B Cab	1	32 ×	75	×38	1¼ ×	3	×1½
(A and B can come from one piece, 92×75×50mm/4⅝×3×2in)							
C Cab back	1	70 ×	75	×25	2¾ ×	3	×1
D Watertank	1	75 ×	75	×50	3 ×	3	×2
E Sides	2	80 ×	100	×19	3¼ ×	4	×¾
F Base	1	310 ×	75	×25	12¼ ×	3	×1
G ladder wheel							
mounting block	1	70 ×	50	×25	2¾ ×	2	×1
Hardwood (ramin)							
H Ladder sides	2	260 ×	12	×12	10¼ ×	½	×½

Drill the centre, then mount it on the pivoting jig illustrated, and slowly bring that down against the sanding disc of a drill which is held in a vice or clamped to the work surface next to it.

As you begin to turn the wheel on its jig, the disc will gradually take off the high spots and eventually produce a very creditable circle.

You can also mount the wheel in the chuck of the drill on a bolt with nuts and washers either side.

Now you can set set it running in the drill, and bring it up against a piece of coarse sandpaper held on a block, as shown in the other drawing.

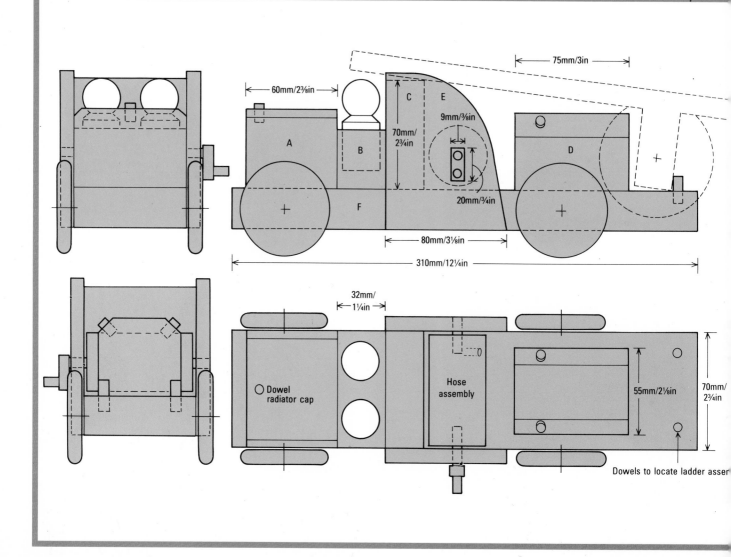

MATERIALS

	Metric	Imperial
Dowel:	850mm approx 6.5mm dia	33in approx ¼in dia
for ladder rungs, joins, radiator caps, people necks, etc.		
People	2 50 × 25 dia.	2 ×1 dia.
	× 38 dia.	2¾ ×1½ dia.
Wheels	4 60 dia.	2½ dia.
	2 75 dia.	3 dia.
Heads:	2 balls 25mm dia.	1in dia.
Hose:	1m nylon cord or similar	3ft
Screws:		
Bright zinc r/head 4	no. 12 × 38	no. 12 × 1½
Washers:	4 internal dia. no.12	
Panel pins	25	1

Wood glue, Glasspaper, Acrylic or modelling enamel, Non-toxic paints

TOOLS

Pencil, paper, tracing paper, carbon
Steel rule, flexible rule
Try square
Tenon saw
Jig saw or coping saw
Block plane or bench plane
Screwdriver
Small hammer
G-cramps
Pincers
Hand or electric drill
Bits: 6.5mm/¼in, 9mm/⅜, 12mm/
  ½in flat bit, 25mm/1in flat bit
Bradawl   Artists' paintbrushes

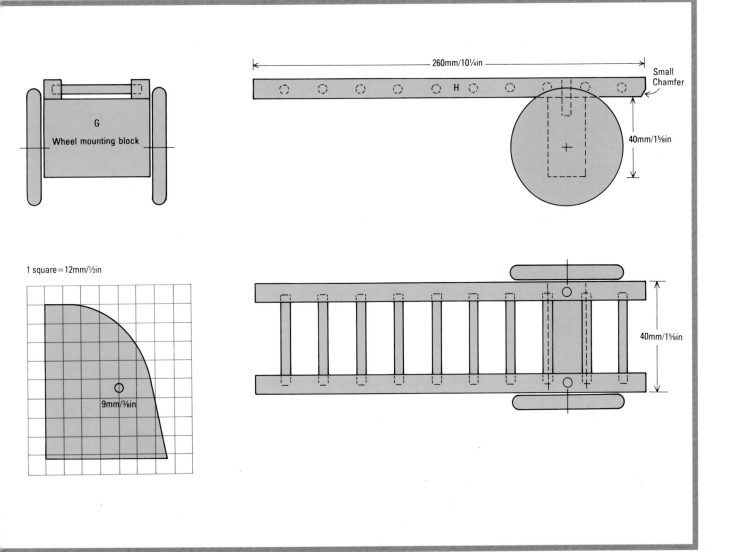

1 Mark, square off and cut to exact length all the main parts A, B, C, D, E and F. Note that the length of the cab back C is across the body – the direction in which the grain should go – and that this is determined by measuring exactly the width of the 75mm/3in nominal timber. For the purposes of the drawing it has been called 70mm/2¾in. Also remember that if you have to use bigger wheels than 60mm/2½in for the body, the body must be longer so the ladder wheels will fit on.

Plane small bevels along the length of the bonnet A and the water tank D. Mark the position of the radiator cap on the bonnet, drill a 6.5mm/¼in hole, cut a 12mm/½in length of dowel and tap it in with a blob of glue. It should protrude about 3mm/⅛in. Draw out the shape of the sides E from your full-size gridded draw-

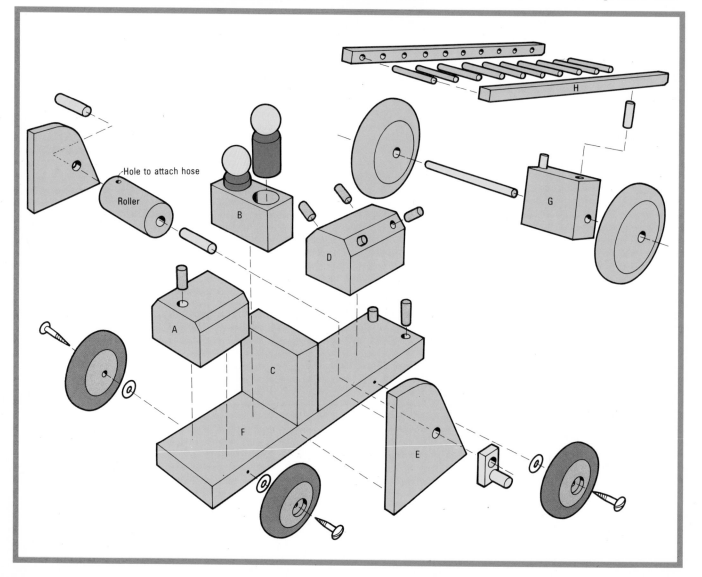

Hole to attach hose

Roller

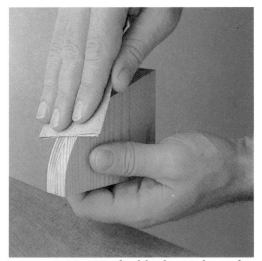

ing, trace it on to the blanks, and cut the curve with a jig- or coping saw; mark the position of the 9mm/ ³⁄₈in hole for the hosereel centres, but do not drill this until the sides are fixed on. Drill two 25mm/1in holes for the driver and his/her mate in the cab piece B (after you have cut it out, if it is one piece with the bonnet A). Make two peg people as described for the racing car, and glue them in.

LADDER

 2 Glue together the bonnet, cab, back and base A, B, (AB), C and F – leave the tank D and sides E until later – and start on the ladder while the glue dries. Cut two 260mm/ 10¼in lengths of the square ramin (12 x 12mm/½ x ½in), and

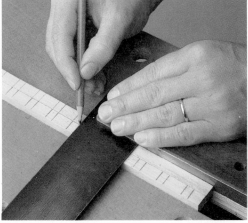

mark 10 positions for the rungs at 25mm/ 1in centres. Mark one piece out fully then clamp it lined up to the other and mark across. Mark 'top' and 'bottom' so they

don't get turned round. Drill 6.5mm/ ¼in holes about 8mm/³⁄₈in deep, and cut 10 rungs 57mm/2¼in long from the 6.5mm/ ¼in dowel.

Drop blobs of glue in all the holes in one side, tap the rungs in, then fit them into the

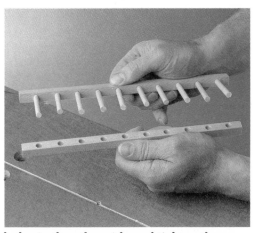

holes in the other side and tighten them up in a vice.

To avoid problems here you must make sure they fit well before you start gluing! Tighten them up in the vice to get the overall width of the ladder about 65mm/ 2⁵⁄₈in.

LADDER ASSEMBLY

3 Cut the wheel mounting block to the exact width of the base (70mm/ 2¾in, but measure it), and plane it to 40mm/1⁵⁄₈in wide. Drill the 9mm/³⁄₈in hole right through it in the position shown on the drawing. Drill a 6.5mm/¼in hole through the centre of the two ladder wheels, cut a length of 6.5mm/¼in dowel to go through the block and both wheels with a bit extra, and glue it into one wheel.

Slide the 'axle' through the mounting block and fit the other wheel on, but don't glue it yet. Now hold the ladder and block up so that the ladder sits upright on its wheels, and mark where the block should be on the ladder, then take the wheels out and glue and clamp the block to the ladder on the mark.

When it's dry drill 6.5mm/¼in holes through the top of the ladder sides into the mounting block, glue and tap lengths of dowel into them, trim off and sand them flush. You can sand these parts and paint them now before mounting the wheels.

HINT
Dowelling as a method of jointing is widely used in toys because it is perfectly safe – no pins or screws to come out. Glue pieces together, under pressure if possible, then drill through both components and tap a piece of dowel into the hole with some glue. It's usual to cut over-length and trim them flush in position. You can buy dowel in lengths, or short lengths of fluted dowel, which are easier to fit because they let the air out of the hole. If you are using smooth dowel, score it with a saw-blade before fitting.

SIDES AND TANK

4 Note that the sides stick out above the cab back to hold the ladder in place. Put a line of glue on the edges of the back C and the right-angle edges of the sides E and pin them in position, but *don't* drive the pins home. One in each edge of the sides is fine. Use your square to make sure the sides line up properly with the body and each other. When the glue is dry, pull the pins out with pincers and drill and fit 6.5mm/¼in pieces of dowel in their place. Trim them flush.

Mount the ladder assembly and judge

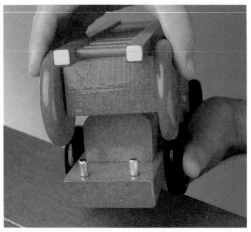

where the locating dowels should be to hold the mounting block, and also how long they should be. Cut them, drill and fix them – too long is better than too short, because you can always cut them back.

Drill and fix two more bits of 6.5mm/¼in dowel in the top and bevelled sides of the water tank D for caps (3mm/⅛in protruding), and then with the ladder in place hold the tank up to the body and see where it will easily go. Mark that position, remove the ladder, and glue and clamp the tank.

Sand all the parts except the hosereel and paint them with two coats of paint.

HOSE ASSEMBLY

5 Paint the inside of the hose area before you fix the big reel. Drill one 9mm/⅜in hole in the marked position, making sure a 38mm/1½in dowel will turn easily inside the hose area; steer the drill across the body perfectly square to go through on the other side. This is best done with the body on its side, because its

easier to drill straight downwards, and if the other side is hard down on the bench it won't break out when the drill comes through. Make the hose crank-handle from a little bit of 12mm/½in ramin, planed down to 9mm/⅜in, and a stub of 6.5mm¼in dowel. Drill 6.5mm/¼in holes in each end and opposite sides of the ramin, and fit on the handle on one side and the hosereel 'axle' on the other. Cut the 38mm/1½in dowel to

fit between the sides with a bit of clearance – about 68mm/2⅝in – mark the centre at each end, drill a 6.5mm/¼in hole, and one in the face for the hose. Now sand and paint the hosereel and handle. Drop a blob of glue in each end and fit it between the sides, held on one side with the handle dowel and on the other with a short piece.

Double over the cord for the hose at one end, put a drop of glue in the hose hole, and glue the hose in. Dip the other end in silver paint for a realistic look.

6 Drill the centres of the wheels halfway with the 12.5mm/½in flat bit, and right through with the 6.5mm/¼in bit; mark the wheel positions with a bradawl, and pilot drill them with a 3.5mm/9⁄64in bit. Screw the wheels on with washers behind them, firm but loose enough for them to turn.

HINT
Panel pins are thin nails which are often used for small thicknesses of wood. It's easier to knock the pin half way into the piece you are fixing first, especially if it is very small; then you don't have to hold it as well as the fiddly bit of wood.

ONE, TWO, THREE...

This abacus is the real Japanese design, known as the 'Soroban'. It has 10 rods, but clerks, bankers and business people in China, Japan and other Asian countries who still use abaci have them with up to 23 rods! Their fingers fly over the special 'waisted' beads, calculating almost at the speed of electricity; but you and the young users of this abacus will be more interested to discover the numerous calculations that can be done with it than to compete with high technology. This is an educational toy, which will help with your child's pre-school learning and dexterity.

The frame is a very simple construction with only five wooden components, but they are joined without dowels or screws by 'open mortise and tenon' or 'saddle' joints. It is important to get the fit of the joint absolutely right – not too loose, not too tight – but if there is still some weakness after you have glued the frame together, you can drill right through and glue a 6.5mm/¼in dowel through all three parts of the joints to strengthen them. A mortise gauge is also useful here, because once you have got it set up you use the same marking for both the mortise and the tenon. An ordinary single-point marking gauge will do, but you can buy gauges with two points on one side for easy mortise marking, and one point on the other.

The use of the abacus is a science in itself, so it's best to get a good book about it from the library. The basic principle is that the rods which are marked by dots carry the beads which form the 'ones' in hundreds, tens and units system.

To make a bead represent a number you push it up to the cross bar; the blue beads above the bar are units of five; thus a blue bead against the bar on one rod and a red one on the same rod hard up to the other side of the bar means 6. Look at the drawing and notice that the beads are positioned on the bar to read from 1 to 0. If you were using more complex figures, the four rods on the right hand end would thus,

MATERIALS

First quality (FAS) softwood (pine): Lengths exact, widths/thicknesses nominal

	Metric			Imperial		
A Frame rails	2 360mm×	25mm	×15	14¼in×	1in	×⅝in
B Frame sides	2 208	× 25	×15	8⅜	× 1	×⅝
C Bar	1 330	× 15	×12	13	× ⅝	× ½
Oval beads	54 22 dia.	18		⅞ dia. ¾		
Rods (welding rod)	10 196	× 3 dia.		7¾	×⅛ dia.	
Hardwood dowel	4 30	× 6.5 dia.		1⅛	×¼ dia.	

NOTE: if you will be turning the beads on a lathe, you will need 6 260mm/10¼in lengths of 25mm/1in dia. dowel instead of the bought beads. They should have 4mm/5/32in holes.
Medium and fine glasspaper, non-toxic polyurethane varnish, red and blue non toxic acrylic paint or modeller's enamel (optional) wood glue (PVA), permanent black marker pen.

TOOLS

Pencil	Drill bits: 3mm/⅛in,
Try-square	4mm/5/32in, 6.5mm/¼in
Steel rule, flexible rule	Block plane
Marking or mortise gauge	G-cramps
Tenon saw	Mallet or small hammer
Chisels: 3mm/⅛in, 6mm/¼in,	Hacksaw
19mm/¾in	Fine metal file
Electric or hand drill	25mm/1in flat brush

taken all together, read as 7,890. Be sure to 'clear' all the beads away from the bar whenever you start a new calculation or go from units to tens or from tens to hundreds.

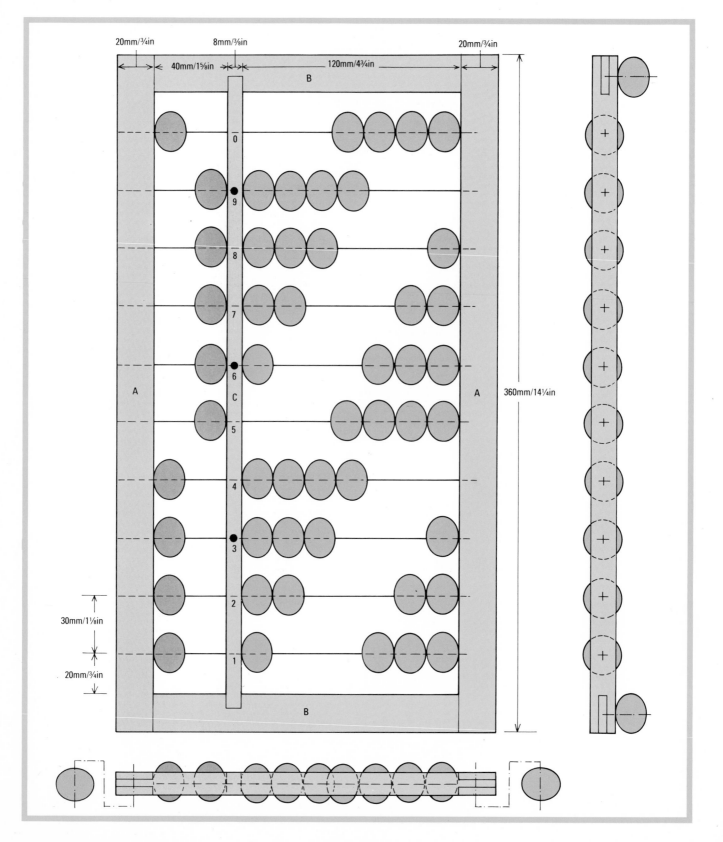

1 Measure and cut all the frame components A and B, but not the bar C. Square off the lines on the frame rails and sides, but the joints will be neater if you cut the pieces 2mm/³⁄₃₂in over length at each end, and wait until the frame is glued together to trim the 'horns'. Holding the pieces together in pairs, carefully mark the 'shoulder' lines of the joints; take the inside measurements of the frame off the drawing for this. Now set your mortise gauge to as near a third of the actual thickness of the wood as you can get; it has been assumed here that 15mm/⅝in nominal will finish to 12mm/½in.

If you use Imperial measurements set the gauge so you get a tenon of ³⁄₁₆in and shoulders either side of ⁵⁄₃₂in. If you are

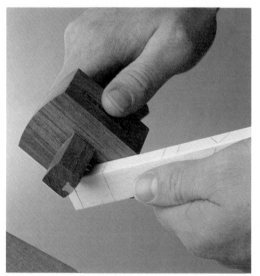

using just a marking gauge, set it to 4mm/⁵⁄₃₂in, and mark along the narrow edges of the pieces and their endgrain up to the shoulder-lines. Pencil in the waste so you don't cut the wrong bits off; the mortises are in the long rails A, the tenons on the shorter sides B.

2 Cut the mortises first in the rails A, carefully with the tenon saw, holding the pieces vertically in the vice with just the joint area and a bit more protruding above the jaws. Do all the cuts, being careful to stay fractionally inside the line, then take all the pieces and chop out the waste with the 3mm/⅛in chisel, starting near the outside end and taking little bites as you work back to the line.

Don't chop the whole lot out in one go, or

the wood will probably break out at the joint line. When the inner waste is removed, pare the sides of the mortises as flat as you can, eyeing it down on to the bench from above as you work with the chisel. If you are not sure whether to take a bit more off or not, don't – yet.

3 Now cut the tenon shoulders in the sides B, being careful not to cut into the area which will be the tenon when the 'cheeks' are removed.

Put the sides in the vice one by one and saw as straight down the lines as you can, erring on the 'safe' waste side if you err at all. When all the cheeks are removed, try each tenon in each mortise for the best fit, then mark the ends of the pieces 'A' and 'A', 'B' and 'B' and so on so you don't lose track of which fits where. Then fit each joint in earnest, paring the tenons first back to the gauge lines, then a bit off the insides of the mortises, fitting all the time. The fit should be snug – the pieces held together under their own friction – but not too tight, or you may possibly split the wood.

4 When everything fits nicely, lay the sides close together on the bench, tops and bottoms matching, and mark the thickness of the bar C across both at the position shown on the drawing, using the overlength bar itself and a square.

Dry-fit the frame together and lay it out perfectly square on the bench, cut the bar to length, and mark off the depths of the notches in the frame sides for it by laying it across the frame and making a pencil mark

HINT
The best way of making sure a frame is perfectly square is by measuring the diagonals. You can do it without a rule by tapping a panel pin in the narrow edge of a lath, setting the pin inside each corner and making a mark on the face of the lath where it crosses the other corner. Push or pull the frame by its corners until the marks you have made match up.

at each end of the bar on to the frame. Take it apart again and cut the notches, clearing them out with the 6mm/¼in chisel. Fit the whole frame together again, and make any adjustments.

5 Turn the beads up on a lathe, if you are using one, from the lengths of 25mm/1in dowel, or take a bead and measure its larger dimension; don't worry if you can only get round beads, it is just that oval ones are better for an abacus. With the bead diameter in mind, mark out on one of the frame rails A the centres of the rods, bearing in mind that they should be equally spaced but that the outside ones are only half the bead diameter plus a little bit from the frame sides.

Take two slivers of wood, hardboard or ply that fit well in the open mortises, and set the two frame pieces together, the marked one on top, with the bar in between them, registered perfectly so the ends overlap the mortises of the rails equally – as they do when the frame is assembled. Use masking tape or adhesive tape to keep the bar in the correct position, and the slivers

of wood in the mortises to keep the frames vertically aligned.

Set the square up next to a mark and drill with the 3mm/⅛in drill through the top rail and bar and halfway into the bottom rail, taking care to keep the drill perfectly vertical in both axes. Someone else's eye is a help here, unless you have a drill stand. A piece of tape on the drill will also stop you going too deep.

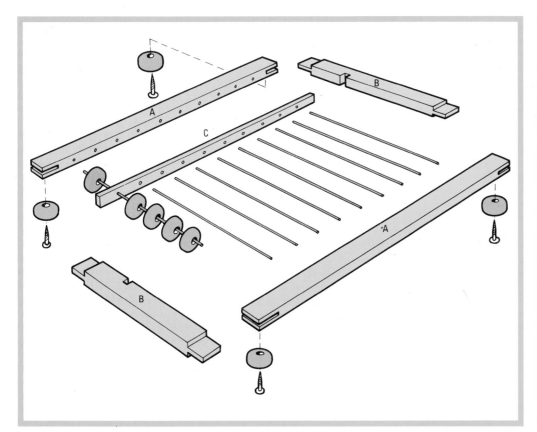

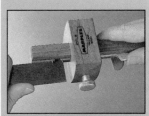

HINT
When using a mortise gauge the stock and one pin must sometimes be adjusted and tightened together. The best gauges have an arrangement which allows you to adjust them independently. Set the pins the right distance apart with a steel rule, then set the stock the right distance from the nearer pin. Tap one end or the other of the handle lightly on the bench to make minute adjustments.

6 Sand all the components with medium then fine glasspaper, then spread glue in all the joints and glue the frame together, using a few over-length pieces of rod through the holes to make sure the alignment is good.

Cramp it to the bench when you have aligned it perfectly square and leave it to dry. When it is set, trim off the overlength horns of the joint pieces with chisel and block plane.

Drill 6.5mm/¼in holes in four of the beads and in the corners of the frame on one side, cut short lengths of 6.5mm/¼in dowel, and glue them into the beads and the holes in the frame to make a stand. Give everything a quick sand again, and then varnish it with three coats of the varnish, rubbing down gently between each coat. If you have used your own turned beads, paint 40 red and 10 blue.

7 Test that the beads slide through the rod and spin easily. If not, make the holes bigger. Cut the welding rod to length, testing to see that it finishes neatly with the top surface of the

top frame rail, and slide the rods through both sets of holes, threading the beads in the right positions as you push the rod through.

Make black dots on the bar where the third, sixth, and ninth rods from the left go through with the permanent black marker pen, and your abacus is ready for use.

GOING TO THE ZOO

This attractive toy calls up images of the travelling shows of middle America, the zoos and circuses that wind their way slowly from town to small town, their Mack trucks thundering, klaxons blaring. It is certainly sturdy, though not perhaps in the same class as a 40-tonner! There are also advantages in the flexibility of the design, in that the trailer can be left as a flat bed if you wish, for smaller children to sit astride it. There's no doubt it's strong enough for that. It is perhaps more charming, and certainly more distinctive, if the cage goes on, with the giraffes' long heads soaring above it, on the long, long journey to the next town.

The trickiest part of this construction is the cage with its numerous dowel bars and the need to get every hole matching right. Nothing looks quite so bad as a cage with wonky bars! The important process is the making and marking of the card template; be sure to mark it 'up' and 'down', since there is every likelihood that it will have slight inaccuracies - which can be doubled if it's turned the wrong way. The top of it marks the bars on the cage rim, the underside of it goes to the trailer bed.

1 Measure and cut to exact length the tractor base A and bonnet B; mark out the 60mm pivot disc G with pencil and compass; cut it out and smooth it to the line. Glue them to the base in the position shown, and drill a 6.5mm/

¼in hole for the radiator cap dowel. Cut it and glue it in so about 3mm/⅛in is protruding.

2 When the glue is dry, drill either side of the pivot disc 6.5mm/¼in, about 19mm/¾in deep or anyway right into the tractor base. Cut, fit and glue pieces of 6.5mm/¼in dowel, and trim them off flush. Now drill a 25mm/1in hole in the centre of the disc, again so it goes right into the base – 19mm/¾in at least, depending on the finished thickness of the disc.

3 Measure and cut the doors exactly the same size, and cut the windows out, using the jigsaw or cop-

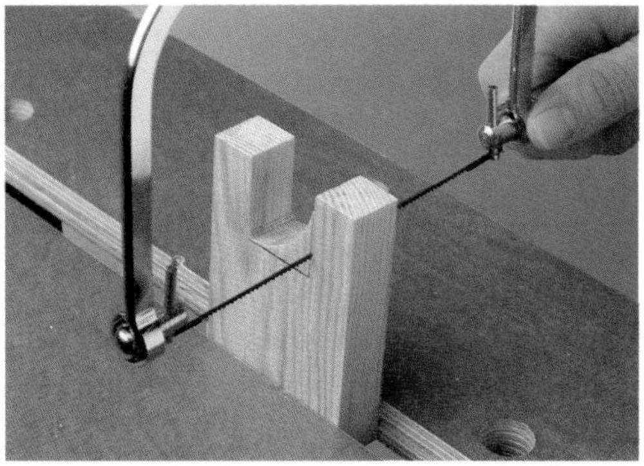

ing saw in the sequence shown, finishing off the bottom corners and edges of the windows with the file and/or chisel. Hold them together in the vice for a perfect

MATERIALS

Lengths exact: widths and thicknesses nominal

		Metric	Imperial
First quality (FAS) softwood (pine)			
A Tractor base	1	225mm× 75mm×38mm	9 in× 3in×1½in
A Bonnet	1	75 × 50 × 3	3 × 2
C Doors	2	100 × 75 ×25	4 × 3 ×1
D Roof	1	115 × 75 ×25	4½ × 3 ×1
E Trailer bed	1	380 ×100 ×25	15 × 4 ×1
F Axle block	1	130 × 75 ×50	5⅛ × 3 ×2
G For pivot disc	1	60 × 75 ×19	2½ × 3 ×¾
Giraffes	1	170 ×100 ×25	6¾ × 4 ×1
	1	220 ×100 ×25	8⅝ × 4 ×1
Hardwood (ramin)			
Cage rim	2	330 × 12 ×12	13 × ½ ×½
	2	66 × 12 ×12	2⅝ × ½ ×½
Dowel		3600mm×6.5 dia.	12ft × ¼dia.
		38 ×25 dia.	1½ × 1 dia.
Wheels	8	75 dia.	3 dia.
Screws: Bright zinc r/head	8	no. 12 × 38	no. 12 ×1½
Washers	8	to fit screws	
Glasspaper		medium,fine	
Wood glue		Non toxic paint or varnish	

TOOLS

Tenon saw	Small hammer
Pencil, paper, tracing paper, carbon	Jigsaw or coping saw
Compass	12mm/½in chisel
Try square	Fine cut wood rasp
Steel rule, flexible rule	Block plane or Surform shaper plane
Hand or electric drill	Screwdriver
Drill bits: 3.5mm/9/64in, 6.5mm/¼in, 12mm/½in and 25mm/1in flat bits	G-cramps
	Bradawl

match. Round off the bottom corners. Cut the roof slightly oversize, then clamp the doors square across on either side of the bonnet/base, put a line of glue on the tops of the window posts, and lay the roof down on them; weight it until the glue dries. When it has dried, drill 6.5mm/¼in holes through each corner of the roof into the window posts, cut four lengths of dowel slightly more than the depth of the holes overall, glue and fit them. Trim them off flush and sand them when the glue is dry. Similarly, trim with plane, chisel, glass-paper and/or file the overlapping edges of the roof so it comes flush with the doors. Round off the roof edges.

4 To fix the cab assembly to the bonnet/base, lay 9mm/⅜in dowels along the base on a flat surface (pencils will do, as long as they are the

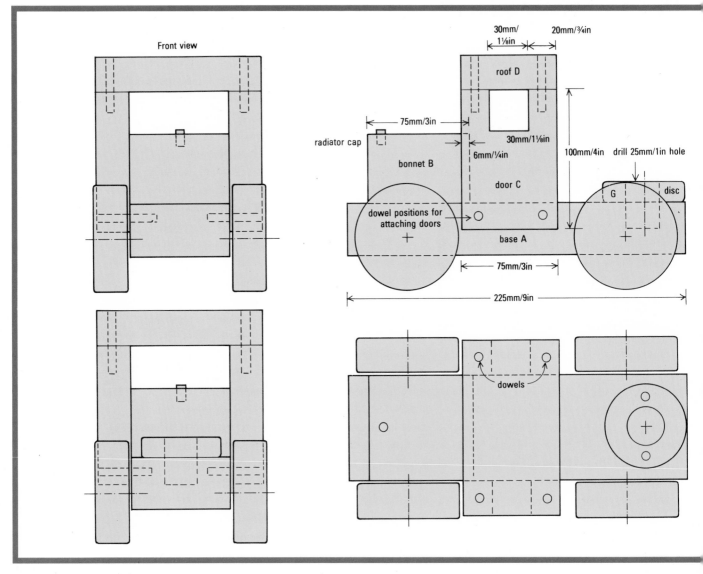

same thickness), put a line of glue along the bottom inside edges of the doors, and lay them down across the bonnet/base with their front edges overlapping on to the bonnet about 6mm/¼in.

Let the glue dry then drill a 6.5mm/¼in hole in each bottom corner, cut, glue and fit 6.5mm/¼in dowels to hold them really strongly. Trim them off flush.

TRAILER BED

5 Measure and cut the trailer bed exactly to length. Mark a centre line a few inches down one end of what will be the underside, then mark out and cut the rounded end. Now hold it over the tractor base and decide where the 25mm/1in pivot can be that will go into the hole in the tractor base.

Mark the centre of the hole and drill it with a 25mm/1in flat bit as deep as you can go without breaking through. It's best here to mark your drill with masking tape for depth.

Mark and cut the axle block F exactly to length, and glue it centrally to the other end of the underside of the trailer, 6mm/¼in in from the end.

Drill for two 6.5mm/¼in dowels through from the top, glue, fit and trim them. Sand everything smooth on tractor and trailer bed.

HINT
If you are putting panel pins through a small section of timber and it splits, snip off the sharp end of the pin with pincers or pliers. The blunt end will break the timber fibres, not part them, and the wood is much less likely to split.

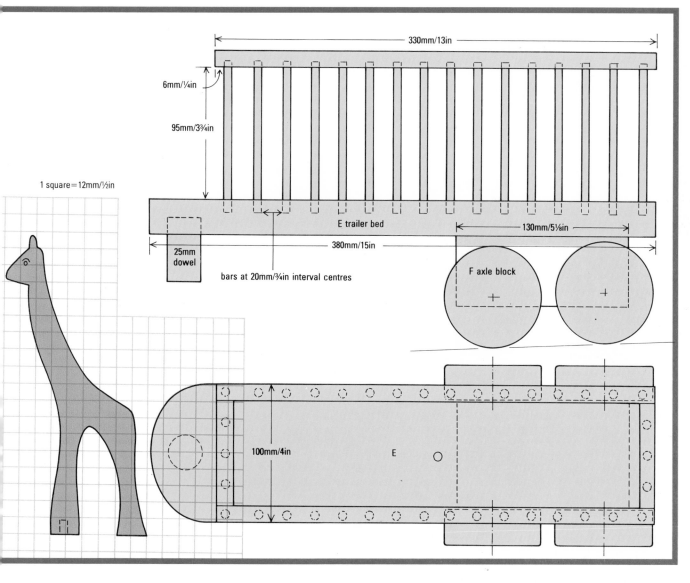

HINT

For a quick solution to find a curve for a rounded end on wood of a given size, have a look in the kitchen for a cup, plate or any other round thing that is similar in radius to the curve you want. Use that to mark round; cheat the ends a little if it doesn't match exactly.

HINT

If you have a large number of pieces to cut the same size, clamp or screw a straight wooden 'fence' to the work surface with an end-piece clamped to it at right angles. Measure from the end piece the length you need to cut, and cut through the 'fence' at the mark; the cut will now be a saw-guide so you just place your long length in the L-shape and cut each piece without having to measure.

CAGE

6 Cut the four lengths of 12 × 12mm /½ × ½in ramin for the cage rim exactly to length, and glue them together with the long pieces over the ends of the short ones. This must be as square as you can get it; hold it with cramps, or cramp down to your work surface over one joined corner then cramp the other two pieces to it. You can pin the corners if you are careful not to split the wood.

7 Make a cardboard template exactly the same size as the rim (330 × 90mm/13 × 3½in if the ramin is dead on size), and mark out the positions of the bars accurately, putting one in each corner to allow for a 6mm/¼in 'underlap', and working on spacing the centres out at 19mm/¾in intervals thereafter. It may be impossible to work out really accurately, but minimise the discrepancies by juggling and cheating a bit!

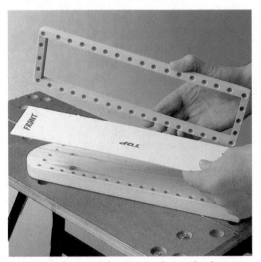

Pierce the template at each marked centre with the bradawl, and mark it 'front' on both faces, and 'up' and 'down' on one each. This ensures you don't transfer errors that the spacing discrepancies might cause. The front of the cage rim should also be marked so you know which is the top and which the underside. Lay the template on the trailer bed and the cage rim in turn – making sure they are all the right way up – and mark through the holes with the bradawl for the centres of the bars. Drill all your 6.5mm/¼in holes as vertically as you can into the bed and rim – 6mm/¼in in the rim and 9mm/⅜in the base. Mark the drill

with tape to make sure you don't go too shallow, which can be as much of a nuisance when you fit the dowels as going too deep and right through the timber. Cut all the dowels 110mm/4⅜in long, blob glue into the holes in the rim, and tap the dowels in. Fit a few dry first and sight them to see they are all going in as far as they should.

Blob glue into all the holes in the trailer bed and juggle all the dowels into their respective holes - it takes a bit of doing, but it can be done! The secret is not to tap one end too far down before the other is engaged. Put the whole thing in a vice and, checking that they are all lined up as straight as possible, gently tighten the vice. Watch and feel if there are any impediments; stop immediately if you feel undue resistance and check out why. Move it left to right in the vice to make sure all the dowels are home.

8 Measure the depths of the two holes in the pivot of the tractor base and the front underside of the trailer. Combine the two measurements, and cut the 25mm/1in dowel about 2mm/ ³⁄₃₂in longer. File, sand and chisel the end of the dowel that will fit into the tractor pivot to reduce its diameter a little and make it an easy (loose) fit, then glue it into the hole in the underside of the trailer bed.

9 Draw up a full-sized grid on paper for the giraffes, transfer it to the 100x25mm/4x1in timber, and cut them out. Shape them with file, Surform, chisel and glasspaper. Drill a 6.5mm/¼in hole in the front foot of each, enlarging it slightly to take a dowel easily; decide where you want them to stand in the truck and drill for dowels in those positions. Glue dowels in to protrude so the giraffes will stand up but come out easily.

10 Sand everything thoroughly with medium and fine glasspaper, and paint or varnish with two coats.

WHEELS

11 Drill to half depth the centres of the tractor wheels with the 12mm/ ½in flat bit, drill through with the 6.5mm/¼in bit, mark their positions on the edge of the base with a bradawl (square a line across to the other side to line them up), pilot drill with the 3.5mm/⁹⁄₆₄in bit,

and fix the wheels with washers and screws. Fix the back pair of wheels on the trailer likewise, giving them 6mm/¼in clearance between the underside of the trailer bed and their tops, and projecting them the same amount behind the block.

Hitch up the trailer to the tractor, and lay one of the forward trailer wheels up against the axle block, resting on the surface as if it were in 'rolling position'; mark the position of the centre through the wheel with a bradawl, and pilot drill with the 3.5mm/⁹⁄₆₄in bit. Square the line across underneath for the other wheel, and screw them both on with the washer and no. 12 × 38mm/1½in screws.

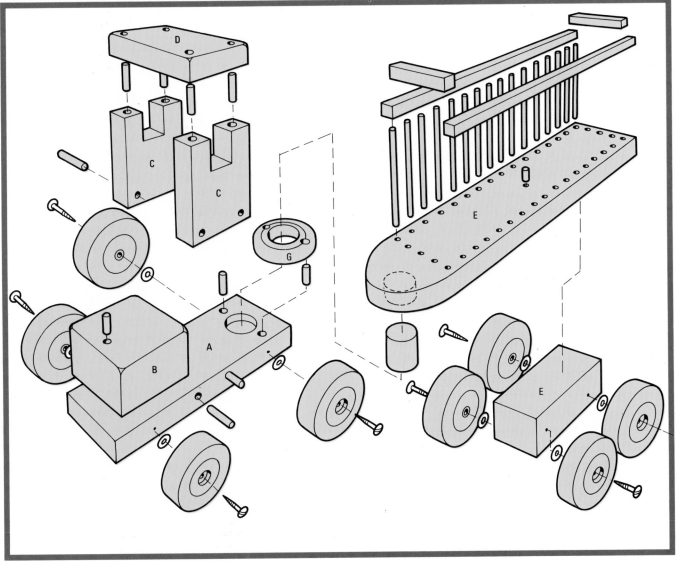

RUB-A-DUB-DUB

There they all are, the butcher, the baker and the candlestick maker, stuck in the middle of the ocean and bobbing about for all they're worth. An imaginative and highly amusing toy that a child, however young, can activate him/herself and giggle at the antics of the three tradesmen in their inappropriate craft. Children of much older than baby age will enjoy this one – in fact we know several adults who remain fascinated! Be sure to fix it up in an accessible place.

This toy is really very easy to make; the skill is far more in the painting, but there is an easy way round even this: if you draw the grids of the various components up full size, ink over the outlines of the people, fish, islands and other bits of scenery, then colour them in with felt-tip pens, you have the picture ready made. Put two coats of non-toxic varnish over the paper after you've stuck it down, and be careful to use a glue (and a varnish) that won't make the paper go transparent. The more confident artists, of course, can enjoy themselves painting in the details and colours. Acrylics will certainly be the best bet here, in view of their quick drying time and the fact that the toy won't generally be getting hard use from sticky fingers – except at the pendulum end.

1 Mark out and cut from the 9mm/⅜ ply the back E, front waves F, pendulum weight G and the bracket H. Draw a full size grid and draw up the shapes, and transfer them on to the blanks

MATERIALS

Ply exact sizes; softwood lengths exact, widths and thicknesses nominal

Birch faced ply		Metric			Imperial		
A Rocker (men)	1	150mm	×150mm	×4mm	6in	×6in	×⅛in
B Cloud	1	77	× 45	×4	3	×1¾	×⅛
C Cloud	1	60	× 32	×4	2¼	×1¼	×⅛
D Island	1	50	× 50	×4	2	×2	×⅛
E Back	1	210	×130	×9	8¼	×5⅛	×⅜
F Front (waves)	1	210	× 65	×9	8¼	×2½	×⅜
G Pendulum weight	1	160	× 50	×9	6¼	×2	×⅜
H Bracket	1	50	× 25	×9	2	×1	×⅜
Beech or ramin dowel							
I Pendulum arm	1	255	× 6.5 dia.		10	× ¼ dia.	
Softwood							
J Spacer	2	32	× 18	×18	1¼	× ¾	×¾
Nail	1	75mm round wire			3in		

Picture hook, fixing screw, two or three small washers, epoxy resin glue, non-toxic acrylic or modelling enamel paints, non toxic polyurethane varnish, masking tape

TOOLS

Tenon saw
Coping saw or jigsaw
Hand or electric drill
G-cramps
Pencil, steel rule, flexible rule

Try square
Tracing paper, carbon paper
Bits: 6.5mm/¼in, 3mm/⅛in
Artists' paintbrushes

with tracing paper and carbon.

Drill a 3mm/⅛in hole in the middle of the back E, 50mm/2in up from the bottom edge as shown. Lay the waves F down and the back E on top of them, lining up the bottom sides and edges, and mark through the 3mm/⅛in hole on to the back of the front waves. Drill into that mark another 3mm/⅛in hole 6.5mm/¼in deep. Cut two softwood spacers J and glue them to the

back outer edges of the front waves F, flush with the sides. Drill a 3mm/⅛in hole through the centre of the bracket H as shown, and 6.5mm/¼in holes in the centre of the bottom edge of the bracket H and the

centre of the top edge of the pendulum weight P – both holes 12mm/½in deep.

Rub a dub dub
Three men in a tub
The butcher, the baker
And the candlestickmaker

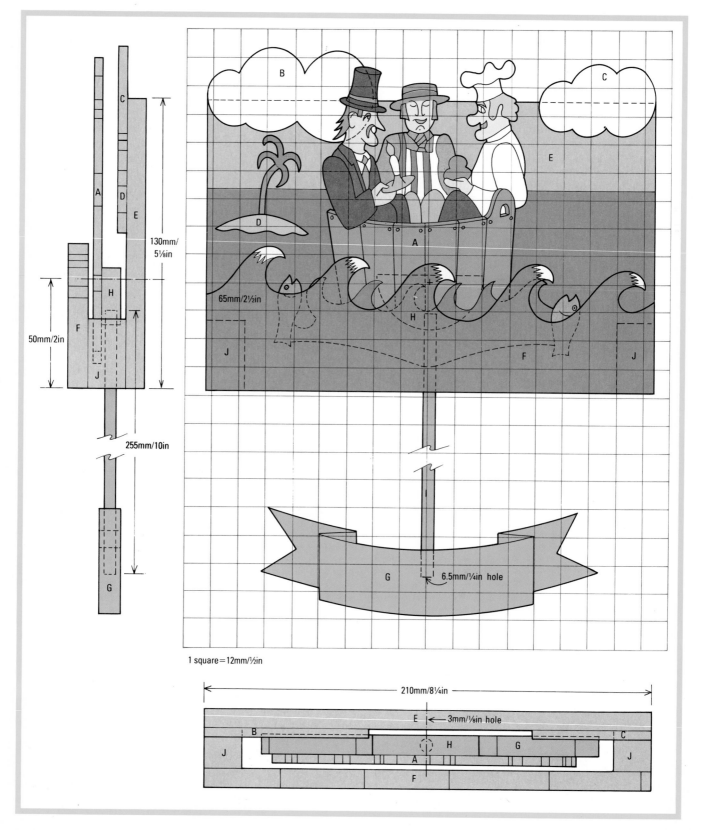

130mm/
5⅛in

50mm/2in

255mm/10in

65mm/2½in

6.5mm/¼in hole

G

1 square=12mm/½in

210mm/8¼in

E   3mm/⅛in hole

B

J   H   G   C

A

F

2 Draw up the designs of the men rocker A, the clouds B and C and the island D on the full-size grid, and trace them via tracing paper and carbon on to th 4mm/⅛in ply. Cut them out carefully with the coping saw. Drill a 3mm/⅛in hole as marked on the men rocker A, and glue the bracket H to the back of A, lining up the 3mm/⅛in holes and making sure the 6.5mm/¼in hole in the bottom of H is at bottom dead centre.

3 Cut the pendulum dowel I to length; now sand and paint all the parts, with either acrylic and then varnish, or first varnish followed by non toxic model enamels. Mask off the joins of the colour areas so one won't bleed into another, and wait for one area to dry before you do its neighbour. Get a straight line on the horizon and the stripes on the pendulum with masking tape.

Write the rhyme on the pendulum weight with drawing ink.

4 Glue the pendulum into the bracket on the back of the rocker/men at one end and into the hole in the

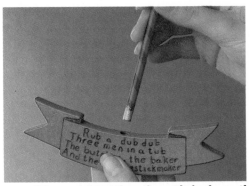

top of the weight at the other. Slide the nail through the hole and check it for free swinging. Glue the clouds B and C at the top of the back and the island D just below the big cloud C. Glue the front to the back, making sure the holes for the nail are in

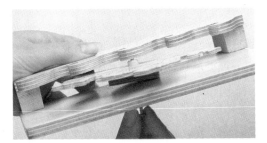

line; have the nail in position while you do this. Cut the head off the nail, leaving about 32mm/1¼in and a point, slide it through the hole in the back, through the hole in the men/rocker assembly, through two small washers, and set it in the 'blind' hole in the back of the front waves F.

5 Attach a picture hook to the back of the back E, and hang it on a wall in an accessible place where everyone can give the men a rock in their tub as they go by.

HORSE PLAY

Medieval renditions of village and childhood life show children riding hobby horses – in fact, the old nursery rhyme has us riding cock-horses to Banbury Cross. Such a simple characterization of a horse still has power over a child's mind, however, and it won't take long for this friendly animal to become a staunch favourite.

The head design allows you great scope for your own sculptural skills to develop. The example shown here has purposely been kept very straightforward, with only a little chamfering along the front edges of the face and ears, but there is no reason why you should not try a more ambitious treatment of the equine features. Your hobby horse can be a docile companion, a trusty steed, or even a noble charger. If you do decide to depart from the design given here, remember to make up gridded paper and draw your own design out on that to get the proportions right before transferring it on to the wood; also remember that it's best to keep the maximum width across the grain to 150mm/6in, as timber in greater widths is more prone to warping.

You can choose to make your own wheels from good quality pine (the size on the materials list is a blank to cut the round out of), or you can use 'hobby' 75mm/3in wheels. Either way the axle must be strong, and the best way of fixing the wheels is with a proprietary 'spring washer/dome cap' system, designed specially for toy-making, and available from hobby shops and mail order suppliers. See the horse and cart for details.

HEAD

1 Make sure when you buy the thick wood ('six by two') for the head that it is flat. You will have to plane it if it is not.

2 Draw up a full-size grid to the size given on the drawing, and mark out the outline of the horse's head on the tracing paper. Tape carbon over the head blank, then lay the tracing paper over that; line up the base of the neck on the paper with the wood and transfer the outline with a soft pencil or ball-point pen. Don't cut it out yet!

3 Draw the lines of the front and back of the neck across the narrow bottom edge of the wood, and mark a point 60mm/2⅜in in from the back of the neck on that edge. Find the middle of the

MATERIALS

First quality (FAS) softwood (pine)

		Metric			Imperial		
Head	1	200mm×150mm×50mm			8in× 6in×1in		

Ramin dowel (broom handle)

Pole		610	×	25 dia.	24	×1 dia.	
Handle		180	×	25 dia.	7⅛	×1 dia.	
Pole fixing	1	50	×	6.5 dia.	2	×¼ dia.	
Wheels							
either:							
Hobby wooden							
wheels	2			75 dia.		3 dia.	
or:							
Wheel blanks (pine)	2	100	×	100	×25	4	× 4 ×1
Axle (steel)	1	92	×	6.5 dia.	3⅝	×¼ dia.	

Washers	4 6.5mm internal dia. ¼in internal dia.

Spring clip-washer dome caps   2 for 6.5mm/¼in bar
Non-toxic acrylic or modelling enamel
Non-toxic polyurethane varnish
Wood glue
Masking tape 35mm/1¼in wide Coarse, medium and fine glasspaper

TOOLS

Pencil , tracing paper, carbon, Steel rule, flexible rule	1in or electric drill with flat bit 25mm/1in
Electric jigsaw or coping saw	Sanding block
Bench plane	Fine cut metal file
Wood rasps and files	Hacksaw
19mm/¾in chisel	Hammer
Surform shaper plane	Drill bit – 6.5mm/¼in
Carpenter's brace and bit 25mm/	Artists' paintbrushes

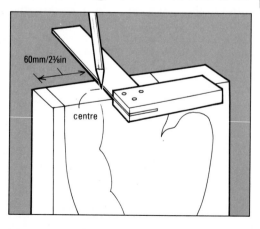

60mm/2⅜in

centre

wood at that point and mark it for the centre of the 25mm/1in hole to take the stick. Mark your 25mm/1in bit with masking tape 50mm/2in from the point, and drill a hole 50mm/2in deep into the head, holding the uncut blank in a vice. The hole must be vertical to the bottom edge of the neck and parallel with the sides of the timber. (See the rabbit mobile for hints on this).

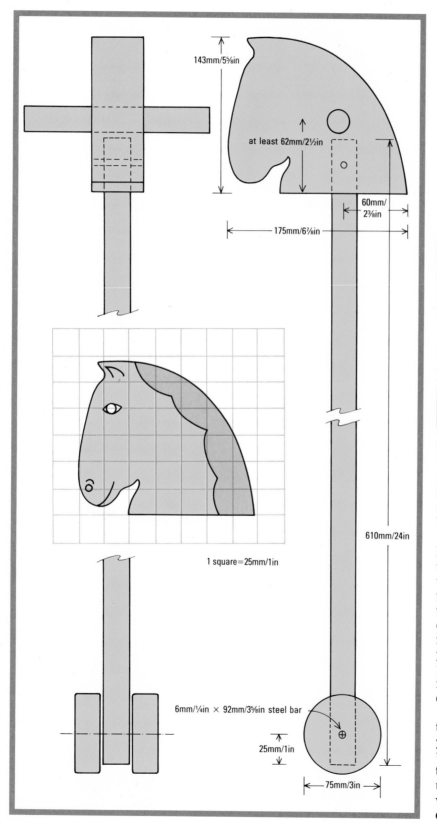

143mm/5⅝in

at least 62mm/2½in

175mm/6⅞in

60mm/2⅜in

1 square=25mm/1in

610mm/24in

6mm/¼in × 92mm/3⅝in steel bar

25mm/1in

75mm/3in

HANDLES

4 Mark the centre of the 25mm/ 1in hole for the handles on the head from your paper template, and check that it does not foul the hole for the stick. There should be at least 6.5mm/¼in clearance.

Drill the handle hole with brace and bit or electric drill and flat bit, checking to see when the first point just shows through on the other side; when it does, take the drill out and finish the hole from the other side. This eliminates ugly 'break-out'. Do this drilling on a surface that can take an extra hole or two!

5 Cut the shape of the head out with a jigsaw or coping saw, taking care to keep the cut square through the wood's thickness. Use the files, rasps, Surform and coarse glasspaper to shape and chamfer the edges, then sand all edges and surfaces smooth with the medium and fine glasspaper.

POLE AND WHEELS

6 The wheels must run in the same plane as the head, so you must fix them to the pole first then glue the pole in and adjust it so the wheels and head line up. If you are using 'hobby' wheels, drill them at the centre, and the pole 25mm/1in up from the bottom of its 610mm/24in length, using the same 6.5mm/¼in drill to match the steel axle bar.

Cut the bar to length and tap it into the hole – enlarge the hole with the drill if it's too tight – then put washer, wheel and washer on either side in that order. Touch up the cut ends of the bar with the file, then tap the spring washer/dome caps over the ends of the axle bar, and the wheels are fixed and ready to roll. If you are making your own wheels, mark the centre of the 100x100x25mm/4x4x1in blanks by drawing diagonal lines, then set a pencil and compass to 75mm/3in and scribe a circle.

Cut round it carefully and shape and sand to the line with files, rasps and Surform until you have a good circle. Now drill a 6.5mm/ ¼in hole through the centres and another through the centre of the pole, 25mm/1in up from the bottom. Mount axle, washers, wheels and spring washer/ dome caps as explained for the ready-made wheels.

7 Now you can glue the pole into its hole in the head; score the part that sits in the head with a saw or rasp to help the glue adhere. Make sure head and wheels are lined up. When the glue is dry, drill a 6.5mm/¼in hole through the side of the head and the middle of the pole and glue the 50mm/2in length of dowel in. Trim it back to the surface of the head with plane or chisel and sand it flush.

8 Mark the centre of the 180mm/ 7⅛in dowel for the handles, and mark half the head wood's thickness either side of that. Spread glue evenly inside the handle-hole, having roughened the gluing area of the handle slightly; tap the handle into the hole so the marks line up on either side of the head.

Wipe off the glue that has spread on to one side of the handle quickly with a warm damp cloth, and sand both sides of it when the glue is dry.

PAINTING

9 Paint the horse, pole and handles yellow, and put the red details on when the yellow has dried. Cut the detail patterns from your full-size gridded template; trace them via tracing paper on to thin card, cut it out and draw round the card. Then paint in the details with a fine brush and a steady hand! The stripes on

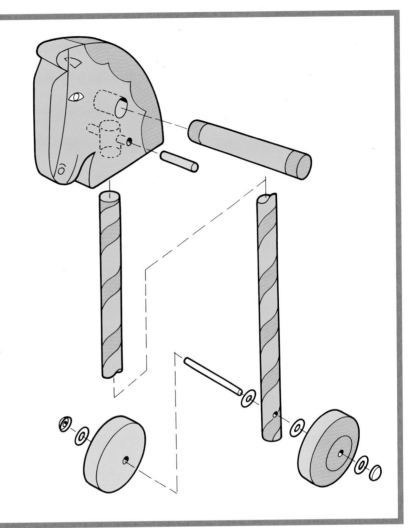

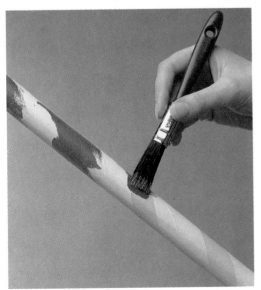

the pole are painted between masking tape, which you must apply very carefully for an even distance between the stripes;

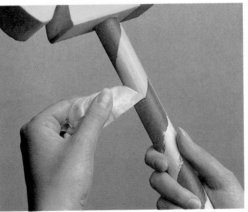

also make sure the edges of the tape are well stuck down, because paint can creep under it. Finish the whole thing with two coats of polyurethane varnish, rubbed down between coats.

HINT
When you cut irregular shapes out of wood, you are cutting along and across the grain. Work your design out with an eye for the grain — the most 'long grain' you can get, the stronger the piece will be. Short-grained corners are inevitable with something like the horse, but the general grain direction must run from the nose to back of the neck.

BABY BULLDOZER

This sturdy bulldozer will be a great favourite on the beach, in sandpits or the garden – anywhere where there's some sand, gravel or just plain earth to push about.

The raise-and-lower shovel is a particularly charming feature of this workmanlike toy. Who knows, you even get some help in the garden with it! In any case, it is bound to be popular with anyone who likes strong, sturdy toys built to take a great deal of rough treatment.

You'll need to paint this toy very thoroughly because it's bound to get some hard use – a minimum of three coats is best, carefully rubbed down between coats with fine glass-paper. Use the explanation of how to make a peg person for the driver that comes in the introduction to the racing car; here, he is made with 25mm/1in dowel.

The number of wheels may seem a little daunting at first, but there is an easy way to get them all in line so the toy doesn't rock, and they all do the work – follow the instructions carefully and remember you fix three before marking out the position for the rest.

The 'scotia' moulding for the shovel is commonly available from timber yards and good hardware stores, but other picture-frame mouldings will do as long as they have more or less the right concave front profile. The back will need to be planed off, but you can find 'scotia' moulding which already has a flat back.

MATERIALS

Lengths exact; widths and thicknesses nominal

First quality (FAS) softwood (pine)

		Metric			Imperial		
A Base	1	230mm	×100mm	×32mm	9in×	4in×	1¼in
B Bonnet	1	140	× 75	×50	5½×	3	×2
C Cab	1	50	× 75	×38	2 ×	3	×1½
D (Scotia hardwood moulding) shovel	1	150	× 50	×50	6 ×	2	×2
E Shovel arms	2	120	× 25	×12	4¾×	1	×½
F Shovel support	1	75	× 25	×12	2⅞×	1	×½

Wheels	6	60 dia.	2½ dia.
Wooden ball	1	25 dia.	1 dia.
Dowel: driver		60 ×25 dia.	2½× 1 dia.
chimney		25 ×12 dia.	1 ×½ dia.

Screws: Bright

zinc r/head	6	no. 12 ×38	no. 12 × 1½
	2	no. 10 ×25	no. 10 × 1
	2	no. 8 ×25	no. 8 × 1
Steel csk	1	no. 8 ×19	no. 8 × ¾

Washers:

	2	no. 10 internal dia.
	6	no. 12 internal dia.

Panel pins	25mm	1in

Glasspaper, medium and fine
Wood glue   Non-toxic acrylic or modellng enamel paints

TOOLS

Pencil, paper, tracing paper
Steel rule, flexible rule
Try square
  Tenon saw
    Electric drill

Bits: 12mm/½in flat bit, 6.5mm/¼in, 25mm/1in flat bit, 3mm/⅛in, 3.5mm/⁹⁄₆₄in
Block plane or Surform shaper plane
Panel pin hammer
Screwdriver
G-cramps
Bradawl
Paintbrush

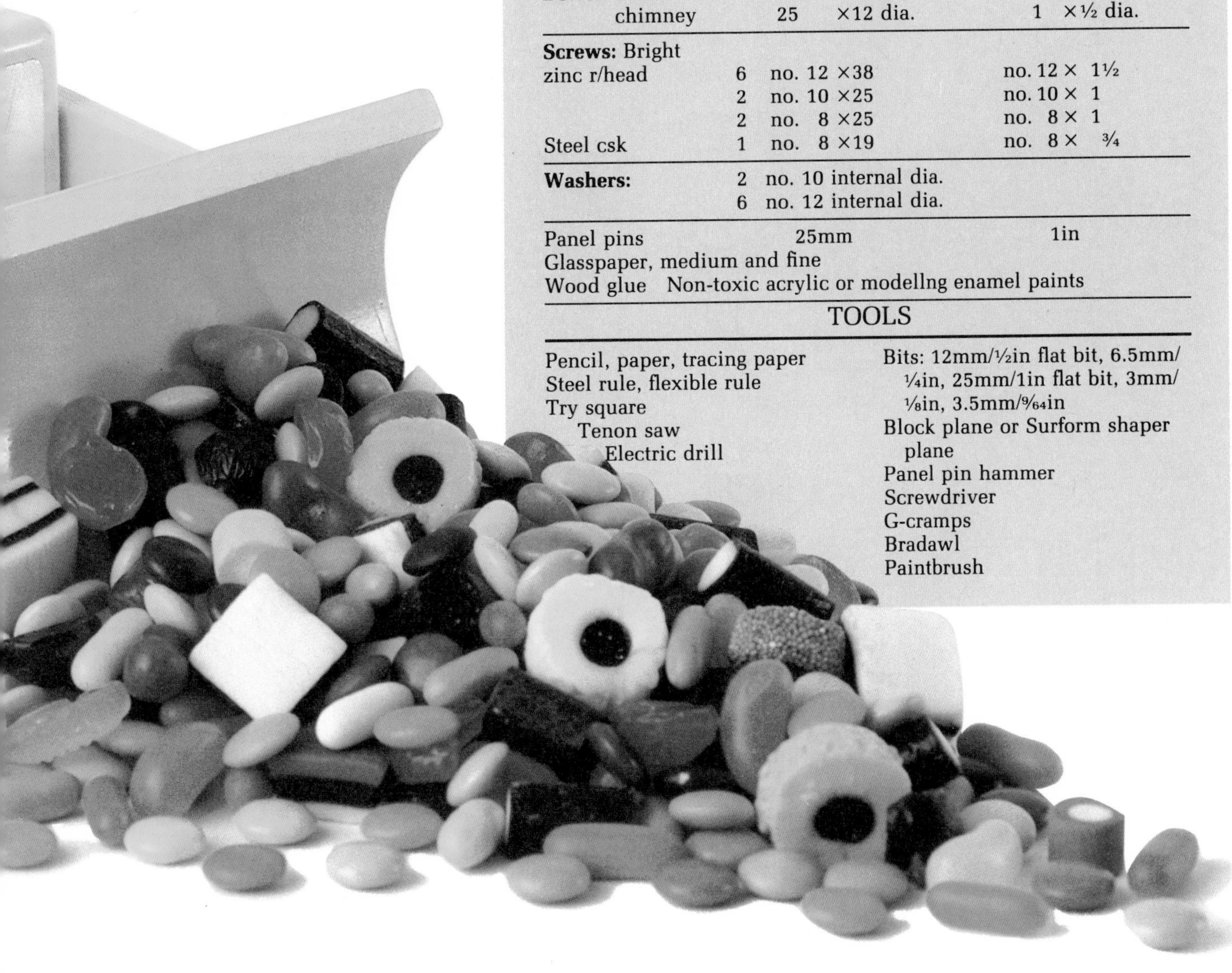

1 Measure and cut exactly to length the base A, bonnet B and cab C with perfectly square ends. If the wheels you have bought are bigger than 60mm/2½in, make sure you increase the length of the base to fit. Drill a 25mm/1in hole in the centre of the cab C, about 18mm/¾in deep, for the driver.

Mark and cut the slope on the front of the base piece A with a sharp block-plane or Surform, and sand all the pieces thoroughly; gently round over the front and top edges of the bonnet B and cab C, and glue them centrally to the base A. When the glue is dry, mark and drill the 12mm/½in hole for the chimney, cut the 12mm/½in dowel and

fit it; sand it if it is too tight. Put a blob of glue in the hole and tap the dowel in; it should project about 18mm/¾in.

SHOVEL

2 Cut the scotia moulding for the shovel D to length and plane the back corner off as shown in the drawing. Then cut the two shovel arms E to length and plane them to shape as in the drawing; drill the central 6.5mm/¼in hole in one end before you shape it so you can measure the centre accurately.

Measure the width of the bonnet (it will be around 70mm/2¾in), and cut the shovel support F 2mm/3⁄32in longer than that. Drill

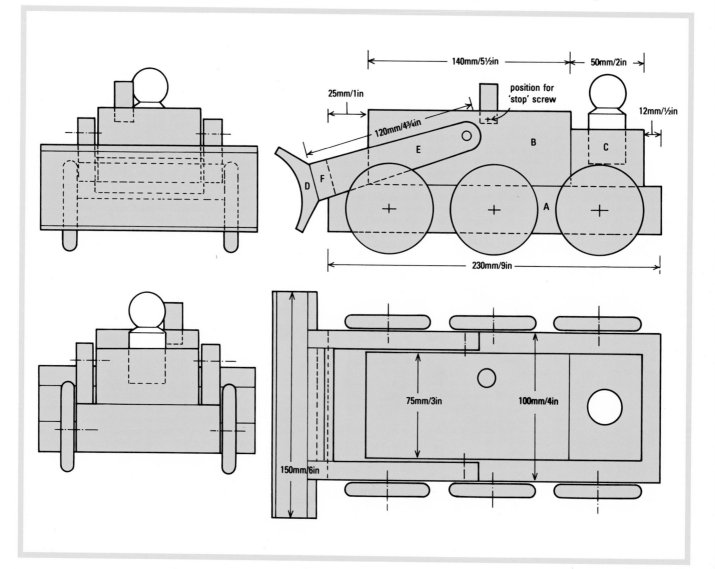

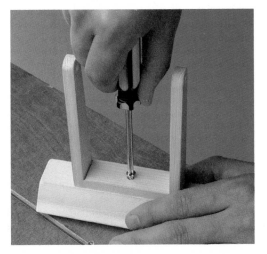

a 5mm/³⁄₁₆in clearance hole in the middle of F, then glue and cramp the arms and support together with the support between the ends, *not* on top of them. Hold the assembly up to the shovel D and centre it; mark through the hole with a bradawl, and drill a 3mm/⅛in pilot hole in the back of the shovel. Glue and screw the support assembly to the back of the shovel with the no. 8 × 19mm/³⁄₄in screw.

3 Make up the peg driver with the 25mm/1in dowel and ball, as explained in the introduction to the racing car on page 69.

Glue him into position in his seat inside the bulldozer.

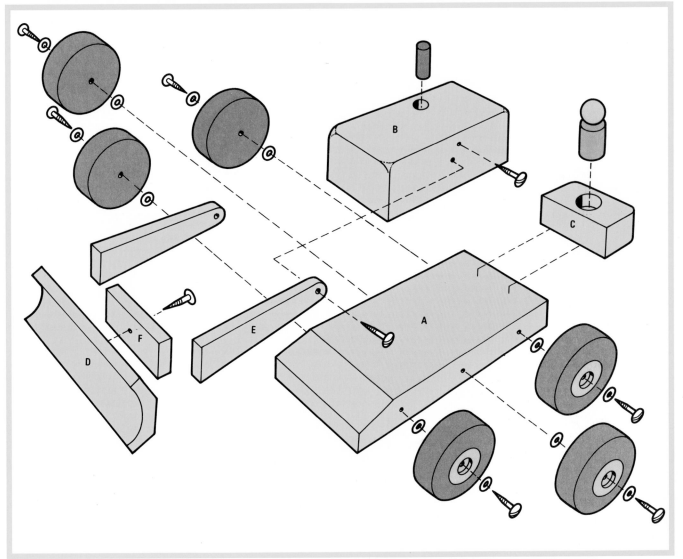

HINT
Most mouldings come in hardwood (often ramin) or pine, but there is a wider range in hardwood. You cannot screw into bradawl holes in timbers like ramin; pilot holes are a nuisance, but a broken screw is worse! If you cannot find scotia, adapt other designs.

HINT
The practice of boring a large hole to a depth to cover a screw head and then going right through with a smaller drill is called counterboring, a version of countersinking. You must be very careful to limit the depth of hole, or the wood left will be too weak to hold the wheel on. Mark the drill with tape to make sure, or better still, use a drill-stand with a depth-stop.

4 Drill the centres of the wheels to half their thickness with the 12mm/½in drill, then sand everything thoroughly and paint all the pieces, including the wheels. Use three coats of paint, rubbing down lightly between each coat for a good key for the next one.

FIXING THE SHOVEL

5 Line up the shovel against the bonnet with the bottom edge of the arms parallel to the slope on the front of the base, and mark the position of the screw hole on the side of the bonnet

with the bradawl. Drill a 3.5mm/%₆₄in pilot hole on the bradawl mark, and screw one shovel arm on with one of the bright zinc no.10 × 25mm/1in screws, not forgetting the washer in between the arm and the bonnet.

Square up the shovel assembly on the body, line it up correctly for height, and drill the 3.5mm/%₆₄in pilot on the other side; screw in the other no.10, and then tighten both screws enough to hold the arm in any position, but loose enough for the arm to move. Move the shovel arms up to

vertical and mark the position of their back edges against the bonnet; pilot drill with the 3mm/⅛in drill, and screw the two no.8 × 25mm/1in in to act as 'shovel stops'.

ATTACHING THE WHEELS

6 Drill 6.5mm/¼in holes right through the wheel centres, where you have already drilled the 12mm/½in holes half depth to sink the screw-heads. Now set the body up on a piece of scrap, a book or anything that is just the height the toy will be when the wheels are on. Mark through the centre of a wheel into the edge of the base at one corner with the bradawl, and repeat this for two other corners. Drill the 3.5mm/%₆₄in pilot holes in these three, and fix three wheels with the no. 12 screws — remembering the washers behind the wheels!

Hold the body firmly on its three wheels

and mark through the centre of another at the fourth corner with the bradawl. Pilot drill and screw the fourth one in, and the bulldozer will not rock or roll. Mark through the middle wheel positions on either side, and fix the last two wheels and washers. Make sure the screws are firm.

WEIGHTS AND MEASURES

These scales are not really a toy, they are the real thing. They can weigh up to 4kg (8¾lbs) with an accuracy of plus or minus 50g (2oz), and aside from giving their young users a solid understanding of weights, measures and balances, they are good-looking and stylish enough to grace any shop of the imagination.

To use them, place the things you want to weigh on the tray and slide the balance up to it along the arm to the point of balance; you can calibrate them in kilograms or pounds and ounces, but the design is based here on metric weights. If the pointer will not balance level, pointing directly at the arrow you paint on the main stand, then extra weights need to be added to the balance weight pin at the end, and the sliding balance re-adjusted. For Imperial weights, the pieces of mild steel you use should be sized so they weigh 1lb; you can then stick two, three or four together for 2, 3 and 4lb weights. If the sizes are significantly different from the ones given here – which in the case of the weights on the sliding balance would affect the component sizes – then try thicker or thinner steel, so the difference is made up in thickness rather than area.

The brass tube required for the bearings will be available from a good hardware store, or you can use copper pipe from a plumber's merchant; be sure to get the right drill for the outside diameter, after you have established the inside diameter fits the roofing bolts you need for pivots. These are available from a builder's merchant. The steel for the weights you can get from an engineer's supplier, metals factor, or even a small engineering shop.

1 Draw up full-size grids for all the parts; the cutting diagram shows how you can get all the parts of 12mm/½in ply out of one sheet 650 × 330mm/25⅝x13in. However you do it, mark all the shapes out carefully, paying particular attention to the positions of the holes where the pivot bolts will go in the

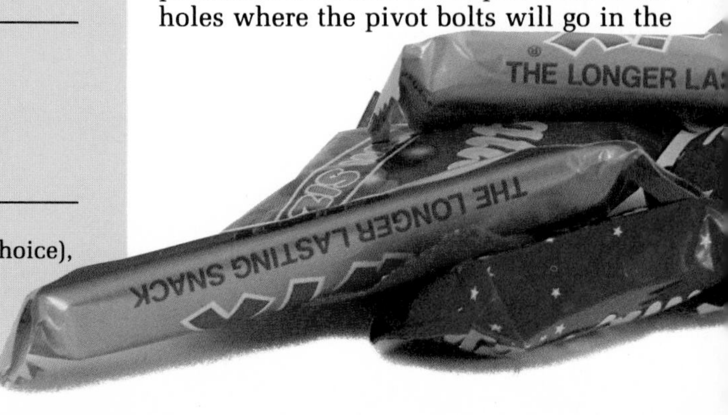

MATERIALS

Best birch plywood		Metric			Imperial		
A Tray	1	160mm	×160mm	×12mm	6¼in	× 6¼in	× ½in
B Tray bracket	1	80	× 40	×12	3⅛	×1⅝	×½
C Tray arm	1	186	× 40	×12	7⅜	×1⅝	×½
D Main stand	1	245	×180	×12	9⅝	×7⅛	×½
E Base bracket	1	230	× 40	×12	9	×1⅝	×½
F Base	1	170	× 72	×12	6¾	×2⅞	×½
G Balance arm	1	436	× 40	×12	17⅛	×1⅝	×½
H Pointer	1	150	× 30	×12	6	×1⅛	×½
I Balance arm stabilizer	1	90	× 30	×12	3½	×1⅛	×½
J Pointer stabilizer	1	90	× 30	×12	3½	×1⅛	×½
L Balance backplate	1	85	× 50	× 4	3⅜	×2	×³⁄₁₆
M Balance spacers	2	50	× 13	×12	2	× ½	×½
N Top balance keeper	1	50	× 18	× 4	2	× ¾	×³⁄₁₆
O Bottom balance keeper	1	50	× 35	× 4	2	×1⅜	×³⁄₁₆
P Balance pointer	1	40	× 25	× 4	1⅝	×1	×³⁄₁₆

Hardwood dowel							
K Weight keep	1	50	×	9 dia.	2	× ⅜ dia.	
S Balance weight pin	1	120	×	9 dia.	4¾	× ⅜ dia.	
T Tray arm stop	1	25	×	6 dia.	1	× ¼ dia.	

Mild steel plate							
Q Balance weights	4	50	× 16	× 4	2	× ⅝	×³⁄₁₆
R Main weights	7	75	× 50	× 4	3	×2	×³⁄₁₆

Brass tube						
U Bearings	4	12	×6 internal dia.	½ × ¼ interna l dia.		

Bolts						
roofing bolts	4	M6	×	50	¼ Whitworth	×2
nuts	12 to fit above				to fit above	
washers	12 to fit above				to fit above	

Screws						
Twinfast (sharp thread) csk	2	no.	8 × 32		no. 8 ×1¼	
	5	no.	85 × 25		no. 8 ×1	
	1	no.	6 × 25		no. 6 ×1	
	1	no.	4 × 20		no. 4 ×¾	
	6	no.	4 × 12		no. 4 ×½	

Medium and fine glasspaper,
non-toxic polyurethane clear varnish (matt, satin or gloss to choice),
permanent black marker pen,
red and white modeller's enamels or acrylics,
wood glue (PVA), impact adhesive or epoxy resin glue

TOOLS

Pencil, paper, tracing paper, carbon	Chisels: 6mm/¼in, 12mm/½in, 19mm/¾in
Steel rule, flexible rule	Screwdriver
Try square	Pliers and/or adjustable spanner
Electric jigsaw and/or coping saw or fretsaw	Electric or hand drill
Tenon saw	Drill bits: 2mm/³⁄₃₂in, 3mm/⅛in, 5mm/³⁄₁₆in, 6mm/¼in, 7mm/⁹⁄₃₂in, 18mm/¾in flat bit
Hacksaw	
Centre punch	G-cramps
Fine files for wood and metal	Fine artist's paintbrush
Block plane or Surform shaper plane	25mm/1in flat brush

tray arm C, main stand D, and balance arm G. The sizes of the holes are noted on the drawing. Cut all the parts out, fairly roughly first with the jigsaw, then trim them to the lines and make the notches neat with coping saw and chisel. Drill all the marked holes. You will see that the bolt holes in the inside faces of the pointer H

and its stabilizer J are recessed to carry the extra lock-nut for the pivot bolts; drill half the thickness of these pieces with the

18mm/¾in flat bit before you go right through with the 6mm/¼in drill. Chamfer the point on the pointer H with the block plane and chisel.

2 Cut the four pieces of brass tube for the bearings U 12mm/½in long, and push them into the holes you have drilled in the tray arm C and the main stand D where the pivot bolts go through. A 7mm/⁹⁄₃₂in drill is given here as the one,

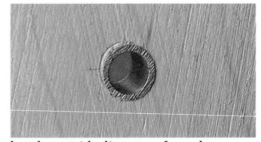

but the outside diameter of your brass may be bigger. It needs to be a tight fit.

File the brass flush on both faces of the arm and stand, and 'de-burr' the inside edges of the holes with a file.

ASSEMBLY – MAIN STRUCTURE

3 Screw the tray A to the bracket B with the no. 8 × 32mm/1¼in screws, and screw through the edge of the tray arm C where the notch is cut for the bracket into the bracket with the no. 6 × 25mm/1in screw. Screw the base bracket E to the base F from underneath with no. 8 × 25mm/1in screws, and that assembly to the main stand D with two

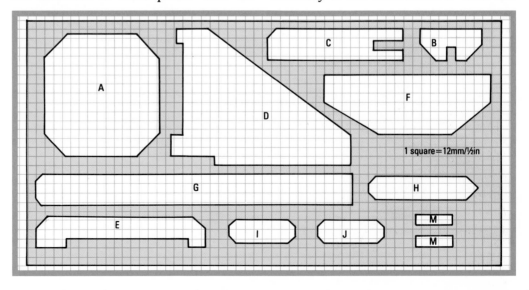

1 square=12mm/½in

more no. 8 × 25mm/1in screws. Cut and shape the 9mm/⅜in dowel for the weight keep K, giving it a smaller diameter for most of its length so the weights will slip on and off easily, and fit that into the hole you have drilled for it in the base F. Only glue it after you have varnished.

BALANCE AND PIVOTS

4 Assemble the balance parts with glue and the no. 4 × 12mm/½in screws, building everything up on the backplate L. Screw the top spacer M to the backplate first, then fix the top keeper N with two screws, and slide the balance on to the arm G. Position the bottom spacer M under the arm against the backplate, and tap the screws through to hold them where you want them when you have got a decent sliding fit on the arm. Screw the spacer and then the bottom keeper O up tight, and screw the pointer P on with one screw.

Cut all the small balance weights Q and hold them together in the vice when you centre punch and drill them through the middle with the 5mm/³⁄₁₆in drill to take a

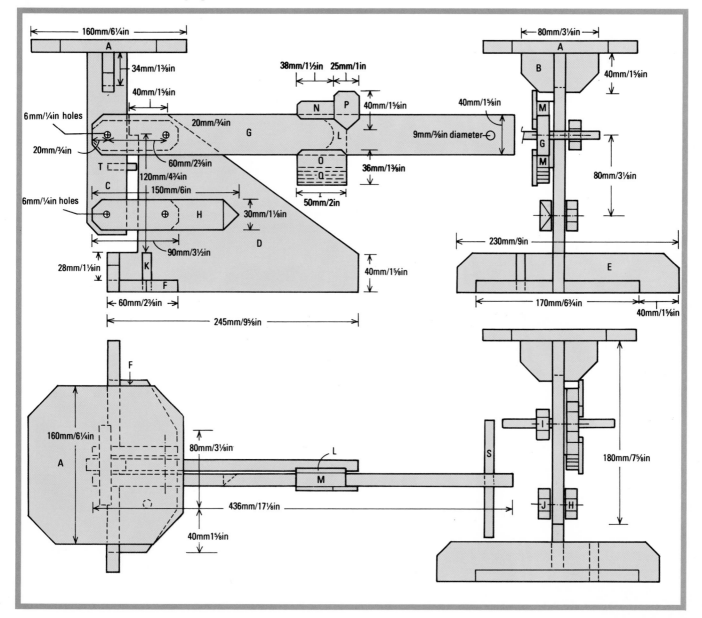

no. 8 × 25mm/1in screw; screw them up under the bottom of the bottom spacer, hard in against the inside face of the bottom keeper O.

5 Using the long roofing bolts, carefully assemble the balance arm G and pointer H through the main stand D with its brass bearings and into the stabilizers on the other side, I and J.

Make sure you have the right stabilizers – J is the one with the recess, to allow the locking nuts to sit flush so the pointer will come up close to the face of the stand and you can judge the position of the arrows more accurately. The order you put the parts together in is: bolt, balance arm or pointer, washer, nut, stand or tray arm, washer, nut, stabilizer, washer, nut. Use the screwdriver and pliers to tighten the nuts round the balance arm, pointer and stabilizers so they will pivot freely on the stand and tray arm. Check that everything moves freely; tighten up if it's too loose, enlarge the holes if it's too tight.

6 Put the balance assembly on the arm and slide the balance weight pin S into position without screwing it. Then test the movement with the weight right out so you can judge the maximum upward travel of the tray, and where you want it to stop; the outer end of the balance arm shouldn't go nearer than about 70mm/2¾in to the floor. Mark the inner edge of the tray arm C where a protruding dowel would bear against the upper notch on the back edge of the stand D – you will be drilling it for the 6mm/¼in dowel T later when everything is disassembled for varnishing.

7 Cut the seven pieces for the main weights R and trim them with the file; stick two and four together with the impact adhesive, and centre punch and drill 9mm/⅜in holes in the centres for the dowels on which they will fit.

8 Disassemble everything, sand it all with medium then fine glasspaper, drill the hole for the tray arm stop T, and cover all the parts with three coats of varnish, rubbing down gently but carefully between each coat. Paint the pointers and arrows over the varnish when it is dry with red enamel or acrylic – if you use acrylic you will have to cover it with varnish again. The other symbols are done with the permanent black marker, but don't put the numbers on the arm until you have re-assembled the scales.

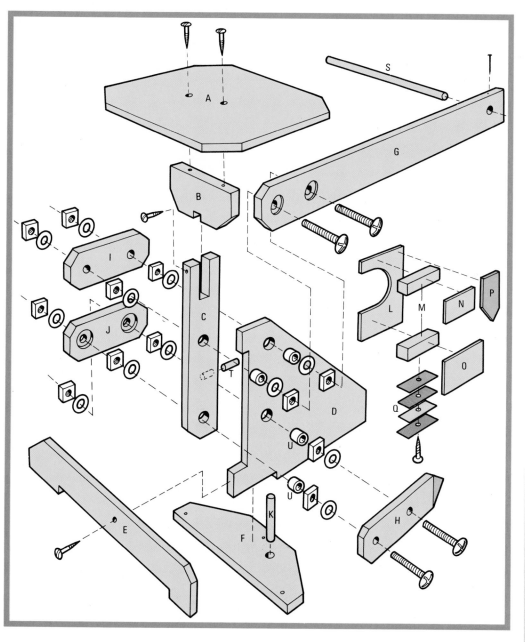

CALIBRATION

9 Assemble the base parts to the stand and the tray assembly to the arm, then bolt the arm, pointer and stabilizers together again, checking that everything still works smoothly and that no varnish is clogging the pivot action.

Slide the balance on to the arm and screw the no.4x25mm/1in screw into the balance weight pin S when it is in position. Now slide the balance right up to the stand, hard against the bolts, and make a 'O' in pencil exactly below the tip of the balance pointer on the balance arm. Slide the balance to the other outer end of the arm so the tip of the pointer is 70mm/2¾in from the end, and mark '5' in pencil.

Take the arm off the scales and carefully divide the distance between 0–5 by five; draw in the markings as shown in pencil, then properly with the permanent black marker. Paint the three main weights different colour enamels, and paint their weights on in white.

DOWN ON THE FARM

This amusing little set is simple to make and will give an imaginative child hours of creative play. Its interest lies in its three independent components; tractor, trailer and person. Put it in a farm or a roadworks setting, and there is the trailer to hook and unhook, things to load and unload from it, the tractor to take the things near and far, and a driver to mount and dismount. He is shown here as reversible with a happy or sad face top and bottom, to be changed according to his mood, but there is no reason why he shouldn't have feet at one end and head at the other, and then even a basic understanding of anatomy can begin!

The wheels are bought from a toy or hobby supplier; the sizes given here are 75mm/3in and 50mm/2in as standard, but as long as the back wheels of the tractor are bigger, it does not really matter. What is crucial is that the height from the ground of the centres of the front tractor wheels and the trailer wheels is exactly the same, or the towing hook will not do its job properly; the trailer will tip back and forth and become an inadvertent dumper truck. Be sure to measure accurately from the base of the two vehicles.

The drawings show how the shape for the tractor with its driver's seat is cut from one piece, which involves cutting 'steps'. This is quite easy with either a tenon or a coping saw; just make sure you drill the 9mm/⅜in holes accurately at the corners of where the seat and 'floor' meet.

1 Square up and cut to length the tractor body A, then mark out for the cuts for the seat, taking the

dimensions off the drawings. Mark the positions in the corners where you will drill holes to make rounded corners. Square up and cut to length the two pieces B1 and B2 for the trailer, and mark on the top, B1, the cut-out and the hole positions in the same way as for the tractor. Also draw a full-size grid and mark out the rounded front end of the trailer and back end of the tractor; then transfer the shapes via tracing and carbon paper to the tractor body A and trailer body top B1.

Cut the rounded ends of the top trailer piece B1 and the tractor A with a coping saw. Then drill

MATERIALS

Lengths exact: widths/thicknesses nominal
First (FAS) quality softwood (pine)

		Metric			Imperial		
A Tractor body	1	190mm×	75mm×	50mm	7½in×	3in×	2in
B1 Trailer body top	1	150 ×	75	×25	6 ×	3	×1
B2 Trailer body btm	1	110 ×	75	×25	4⅜ ×	3	×1

Hardwood dowel

Steering column	1	20	×	6 dia.	¾	×	¼ dia.
Chimney	1	32	×	9 dia.	1¼	×	⅜ dia.
Towing hook	1	36	×	9 dia.	1⅜	×	⅜ dia.
Steering wheel	1	6	×	25 dia.	¼	×	1 dia.
Driver	1	64	×	37 dia.	2½	×	1½ dia.
Wooden wheels	4			50 dia.			2 dia.
	2			75 dia.			3 dia.

Screws: Japanned

r/head	6	30	×	no. 8	1¼	×	no. 8
Brass screw-cups	6	for no.8 screws					
Washers	6	ditto					

Wood glue, medium and fine glasspaper

TOOLS

Steel rule, flexible rule	G-cramps
Coping saw, electric jigsaw	Screwdriver
Tenon saw	25mm/1in paintbrush
Half-round wood rasp, medium	Fine artist's brush
cut	Hand or electric drill
Pencil	Drill bits: 3mm/⅛in 6mm/¼in
Try-square	10mm/⅜in 12mm/½in

PRIVATE
BEWARE OF THE BULL

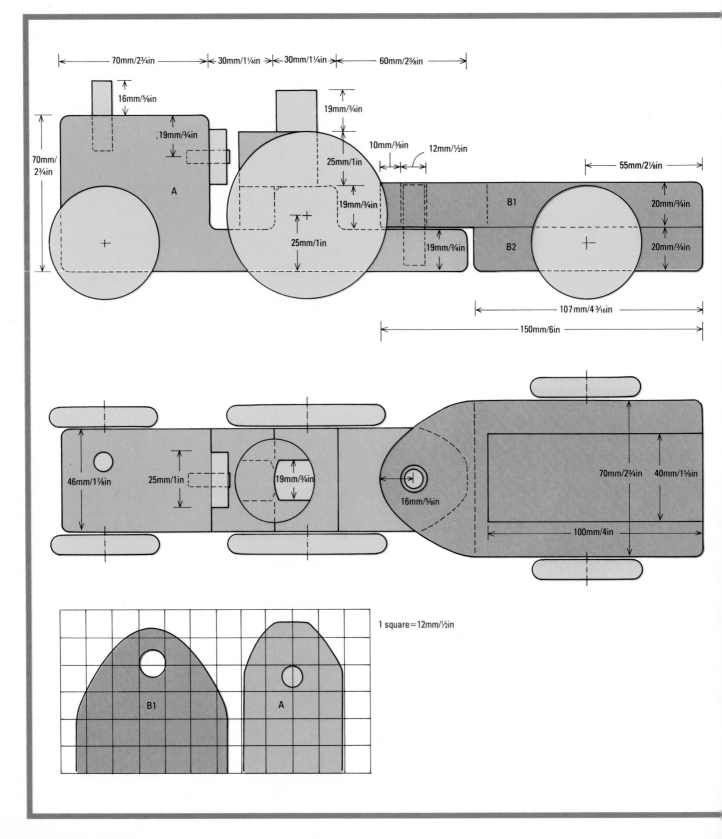

1 square=12mm/½in

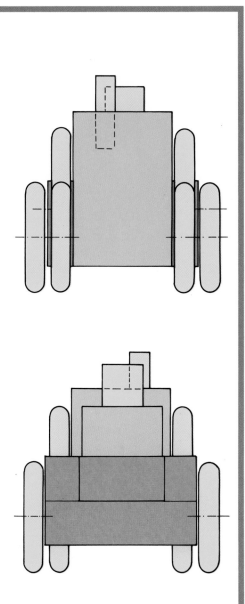

9mm/³⁄₈in holes in the corners of the markings you have made for the seat and the cut-out in the top part of the trailer B1. You can cut the straight back of the tractor with a tenon saw, but the part between seat and steering wheel will need the coping saw; make diagonal cuts to the holes you have drilled to ease the clearance of waste. Make the cut-out in the trailer top, again using a combination of tenon and coping saw.

3 Mark the centre of the 'towing hole' in the curved front of the trailer top B1, and drill a 12mm/½in hole right through. Clamp the piece to another piece of scrap so that when the drill comes through it won't 'break out' the grain on the underside. Always do this for a hole that needs to be neat both sides of the wood. Mark and drill the 9mm/³⁄₈in holes for the towing hook and chimney in the back and top of the tractor, and drill them exactly 16mm/⅝in deep.

4 Mark the position of the steering column and drill a 6mm/¼in hole 10mm/³⁄₈in deep. Drill a 6mm/¼in hole in the centre of the 25mm/1in dowel for the steering wheel. Drill the 3mm/⅛in pilot holes in the sides of the tractor and trailer for the screws that hold the wheels, making sure the ones at the tractor front and the trailer ones are at centres exactly

HINT
To cut exactly the same curve on both sides of a piece without tracing, draw out a pleasing half-shape on paper, fold it, and cut along the curve, the apex of which is on the fold. Open out the paper and you have a mirror image.

the same height from the bases. Mark out and cut the driver as in the drawing, and sand him. Glue the trailer parts together.

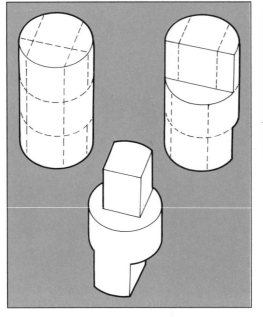

5 Clean up and sand all the components, using the half-round file/rasp for the rough bits and medium

and then fine glasspaper. Wrap glasspaper round a piece of dowel for the sharp curves in the corners.

6 Paint the tractor red and the trailer blue, and the driver's clothes (between his faces) red. Draw the face and/or feet details on and paint them in with a very fine brush; practise first if you find this fine work tricky.

HINT
To drill exactly to depth, stick a piece of masking tape round the drill the same distance from the tip as the depth you want. You can get rubber rings of different sizes for this; watch carefully as you drill and stop when the marker reaches the surface. A drill-stand with a built-in stop is best!

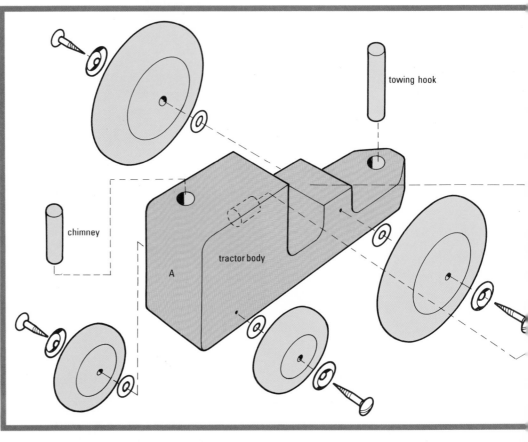

towing hook

chimney

tractor body

A

7 Cut the chimney, towing hook and steering column to length, put a dab of glue on the ends and tap them in to their holes. The steering column should project about 9mm/⅜in. Put a dab of glue inside the steering-wheel hole and tap that on to the column.

8 Varnish the pieces with two coats of non-toxic polyurethane, rubbing down lightly between coats, when the paint is dry.

9 Put a screw cup on a round-head screw, then a washer, then a wheel, and screw it in position; repeat for all the wheels.

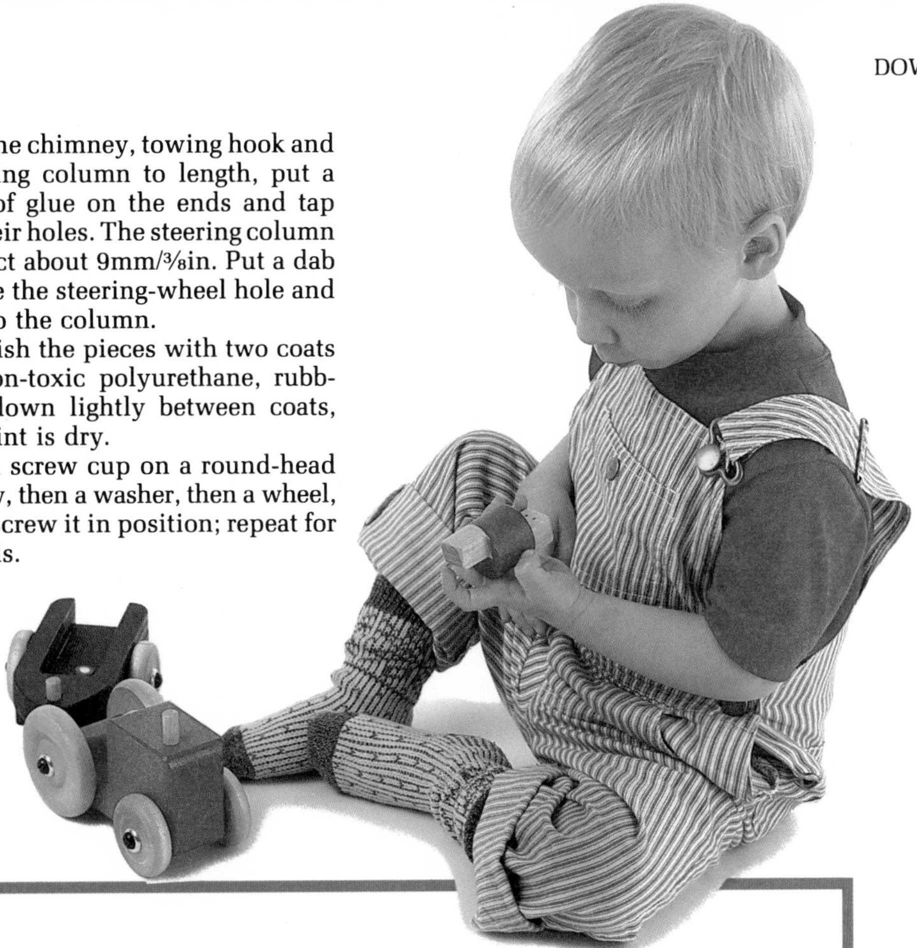

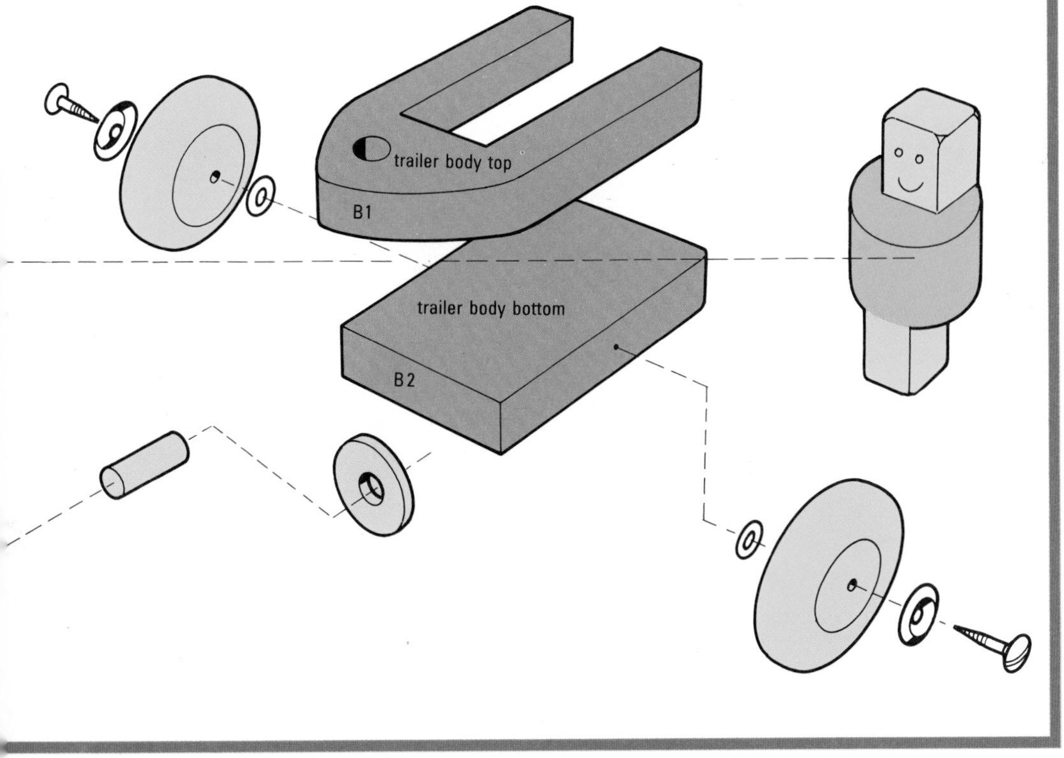

trailer body top

B1

trailer body bottom

B2

HICKORY, DICKORY DOCK

Learning to tell the time, like any other part of a child's learning process, can really be fun — as long as you have a clear, bright and easy-to-read clock for the first introduction. This design, with its brightly painted face, is ideal; it is big, the hands are clearly distinguished in colour as well as size, and it can hang on the wall or stand on its own base. Paint the numbers in big, bold figures easy for a child to identify. If you are something of an artist you could consider painting in the mouse from the nursery rhyme in the title on the clock face for extra interest, or adding some other decorative device designed to appeal to a child of pre-school age.

HINT
Remember when you buy timber from a yard that quality varies widely, and ends are rarely, if ever, square. This is why you should always square and cut your own lines with a try-square and tenon saw to get accurate components. When you are buying, test the wood for weight; with softwoods (pine), a light piece is usually a better bet than a heavy piece because the heavier one is wetter. It will dry out at home and shrink and warp. Avoid knots, splits and 'shakes' — cracks you can see in the endgrain. Don't be afraid to pick and choose.

The painting is perhaps more of a challenge than the actual construction. When your basic clock-face piece is cut to its initial size, the top shape can be cut out; the frame mouldings that go round the face can be almost any profile, but be careful to choose them with an eye for proportion. They do not need to be the width shown on the drawings, but don't make them too wide, or you will throw out the dimension of the

MATERIALS

		Metric	Imperial
6mm/¼in birch plywood. Exact finished sizes			
A Clock-face piece	1	360mm × 280mm	14⅛in × 11in
B Bottom back piece	1	87 × 50	3⅜ × 2
C Top back piece	1	55 × 50	2⅛ × 2
big hand	1	80 × 23	3⅛ × ⅞
little hand	1	70 × 23	2¾ × ⅞

			Metric			Imperial		
First quality (FAS) softwood (pine); lengths exact: widths/thicknesses nominal								
D Upper base	1	280mm ×	50mm ×	50mm	11 in ×	2 in ×	2in
E Lower base	1	340 ×	75 ×	25	13⅜ ×	3 ×	1
F ½-round moulding	1	280 ×	20		11 ×	¾	
G Picture-frame moulding	4	240 ×	16		9½ ×	⅝	
Bead (wooden)	1	25mm dia.			1 in		

		Metric	Imperial
Screws: Steel csk	3	no. 8 × 38	no. 8 × 1½
Self tapping	2	no. 8 × 25	no. 8 × 1
	2	no. 8 × 30	no. 8 × 1¼
	4	no. 8 × 6	no. 8 × ¼

Washers	4	internal dia. for no.8 screws	
Brass screw-cup	1	no. 8	

Non-toxic acrylic paints; red, yellow, blue
Non-toxic polyurethane varnish; clear
Wood glue
Abrasive paper, fine grade (F2 or flourpaper)

NOTE: Sizes given for cut components are exact, so always buy more and cut to length. You will be cutting shapes out of the ply sizes. Wood is usually bought 'prepared' to less than the 'nominal' width and thickness given here – but the accurate length is up to you; and most important, buy picture-frame moulding in long enough lengths for the 45° mitres to be cut for each join. Allow wastage for mistakes!

TOOLS

Pencil	Tenon saw
Tracing paper, carbon paper	Sanding block
Card	Coping saw
Scissors	19mm/¾in chisel
Carpenter's try-and-mitre square	Mitre box
Scalpel or sharp craft knife	Hand or electric drill
(A large plastic set-square would be useful too)	Bits: 3mm/⅛in , 6mm/¼in
	Countersink
Flexible rule, steel rule	Screwdriver
G-cramps	25mm/1in paintbrush
Small block plane or Surform rasp plane	Fine artist's brush

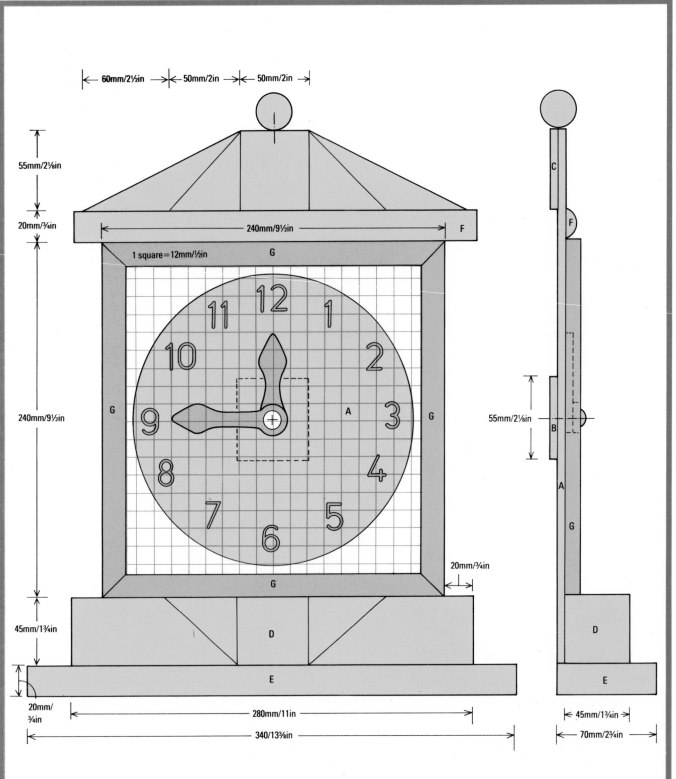

60mm/2½in 50mm/2in 50mm/2in

55mm/2⅛in

20mm/¾in

240mm/9½in

240mm/9½in

F

G

1 square=12mm/½in

A

G

G

G

20mm/¾in

45mm/1¾in

D

E

20mm/
¾in

280mm/11in

340/13⅜in

C

F

B

A

G

55mm/2⅛in

D

E

45mm/1¾in

70mm/2¾in

face itself and the hands.

It is important to have a clear idea of which part goes to which in the construction, and which face of which makes contact, because you must mask these 'gluing areas' off with masking tape when you are painting. Wood glue and acrylic paint do not mix well at the best of times, and at worst the two together can stop the glue having any effect!

FACE

1 Square up the edges of the plywood with a small block plane or Surform. You need at least one perfectly right-angled corner with two straight edges. Mark out the shape of clock-face piece A on the ply, making sure every corner is square and measurements on both sides match up. Draw up a grid and trace the clock hands on to tracing paper, transfer the shape to card with carbon, cut out the card and draw round those pieces on to the ply. Mark out the two back pieces B and C.

2 Cut the large piece out first with the ply clamped to your work surface. You might have to move it for the next cut. Then re-clamp it and cut out the 'shoulders' of the top canopy, either by working both ways with a tenon saw or

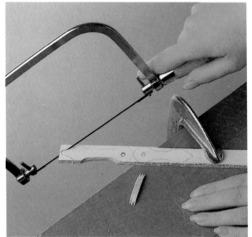

using a coping saw. Cut the shaped hands out with a coping saw, and cut the back pieces B and C. Trim all the edges to the lines with the plane, chisel, Surform, and knock off the sharp edges with glasspaper, held in the hand for curved edges and on a block for straight ones. Sand the flat faces of all the components too.

BASE

3 Mark out the length of the base pieces of softwood D and E, and square lines across at each end on the exact lengths. Cut close to the line with the tenon saw, keeping it perfectly square. Mark and cut the ½-round moulding exactly to length.

4 Cut the four pieces of picture-frame moulding with a perfect 45° mitre cut at each end. Use a mitre box for this. Cut slightly off the line, but

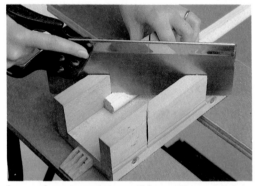

leave the trimming until later. Be careful to get the mitre cuts the right way round at each end, and once one length is right you can mark the other three off that.

5 Sand all the pieces using medium then fine glasspaper; round off all corners and edges except the meeting faces of the frame joints.

PAINTING

6 Mark the centre of the clock face 165mm/6½in from the bottom of the face-piece A and scribe a circle 195mm/7⅝in diameter for the face. Mark out the patterns for the colours on base piece D, making sure the areas are equal.

HINT
The base piece round which you are fitting your pieces of moulding must be perfectly square; 45° mitred angles make up 90°, and when you try to 'adjust' them to fit an off-square angle you will usually only make things worse. You can often 'cheat' a bit if the mitred angles aren't perfect by shuffling them against each other to get the best fit (smallest gaps) on all the corners at once. This will mean they do not match up perfectly with the base you are laying them on, but it is easier and less noticeable to plane the proud edges of that base piece off after you have fixed the mouldings.

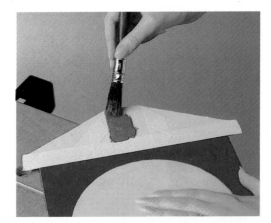

7 When you are painting the separate components, bear in mind where the gluing areas are and keep the paint off them. You can use masking tape. Do not paint the flat bottom of the ½-round or picture-frame mouldings, the back of D where A sticks to it, the bottom of D and top of E where they go together, and the areas of A on to which the various components are stuck. Paint the yellow areas first, (re-marking the clock-face centre) then the red (except the numerals), then the blue.

Allow them to dry, then trace the numer-

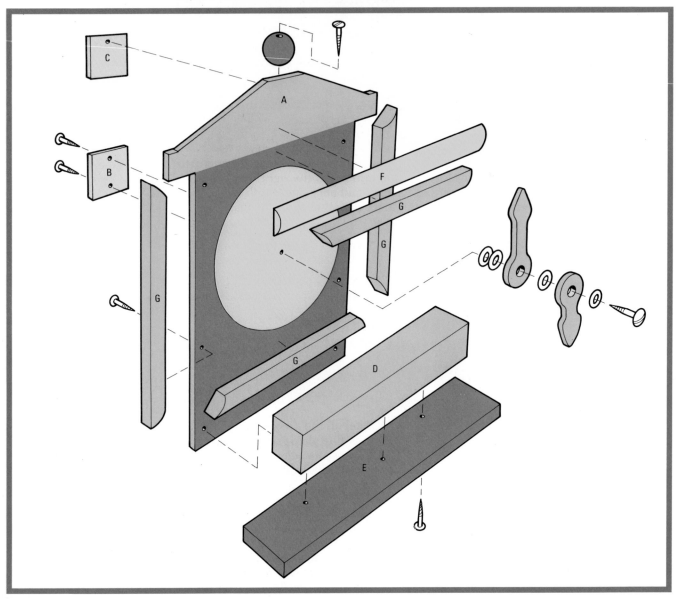

als on to the yellow clock face. Practice this first, then paint them in carefully on the face.

ASSEMBLY

8 Glue the upper base piece D to the bottom of the front of the face piece A, lining up the centres and the bottom edges perfectly flush. Cramp, using soft pads to avoid marking the paint; check alignment, and leave them to dry. They might slip under cramps – be careful here. When this is dry glue the lower base piece E to D, lining the back edge up with the back bottom edge of the face piece A. D supports A upright, and both sit on E.

9 Now fit the picture-frame moulding pieces G to the face. Start with the bottom one that butts to the upper base D, and trim it to exact length to fit the width of the face with plane or chisel. Trim, fit and lay the other ones out dry all round the face so the mitred corners fit as best you can get and they line up round the edges of the face. When you're satisfied with the fit, glue all the pieces, making sure the glue is on their meeting faces as well as the flat bottoms, to the face and each other. Glue the ½-round strip along the top, hard up to the picture-frame moulding.

10 Glue the back pieces B and C as shown in the drawing and allow them to dry. The top one supports the bead and is drilled for wall hanging; the bottom one carries the screw on which the hands pivot.

11 Paint the hands, unpainted edges, and areas you might need to retouch. Don't paint the back of the hands! Varnish the whole thing with two coats, rubbing down lightly with fine glasspaper between coats.

DRILLING/SCREWS

12 Mark the base holes as shown in the 'exploded' drawing, drill 6mm/¼in holes through the lower base E, and 'pilot' 3mm/⅛in holes through the larger ones into the base piece D. Screw the 38mm/1½in woodscrews through E into D.

13 Drill 6mm/¼ pilot holes in the back of the face piece A to fix screws through to D and the frame pieces G. Drill the same size holes in the

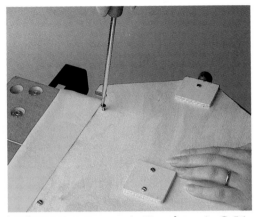

backing pieces – two in B and two in C. It's absolutely vital you don't drill too far through the face and out the other side of the frame pieces. Drill a 6mm/¼in hole in the top backing piece C for the clock to hang on a nail on the wall.

14 With the clock face down on a soft cloth to protect the paint, fix A to D with the two 25mm/1in self-tapping screws, and screw through the back with 6mm/¼in self-tapping screws into the frame pieces and through the backing pieces into the face piece. Screw one 30mm/1¼in through the bead into the top of backing piece C. Drill a 3mm/⅛in hole to 10mm deep in the centre of the face.

FIXING THE HANDS

15 Put the screw cup on the other 30mm/1¼in screw, then the big hand, a washer, the small hand, and the other washers, in that order. Care-

fully screw the whole assembly into the central hole, tight enough to hold the hands in any position but not so tight they won't turn!

VINTAGE VAN

This sturdy and elegant toy is not only modelled on the design of an actual vintage truck, but also the design of a vintage toy! Children in the 1920s and 30s pushed them around, drove them on delivery rounds, sat on them, and stored all manner of fascinating objects in them, just as they will today. The van is ideal for out of doors, with its strong plastic wheels and steel axles – only be sure that no one gets the idea it's a good mount to ride down a hill on, since there is no steering!

MATERIALS

Lengths exact; widths and thicknesses nominal for softwood

First quality (FAS) softwood (pine)

		Metric			Imperial		
A Lower base	1	405mm	×150mm	×25mm	16in×	6in	×1in
B Upper base	1	250	×150	×25	10 ×	6	×1
C Bulkhead	1	152	×150	×25	6 ×	6	×1
D Engine bulkhead	1	82	×150	×25	3¼×	6	×1
I Engine top	1	100	× 75	×25	4 ×	3	×1
J Doors	2	150	× 75	×25	6 ×	3	×1
N Outer front wing	2	115	× 75	×25	4½×	3	×1
K Engine side	2	75	× 50	×25	3 ×	2	×1
L Engine front	1	56	× 50	×25	2³⁄₁₆×	2	×1
M Inner front wing	2	95	× 50	×25	3¾×	2	×1
P Rear roof support	1	150	× 25	×25	6 ×	1	×1
Q Front axle bearer	2	65	× 25	×25	2½×	1	×1
R Rear axle bearer	2	75	× 25	×25	3 ×	1	×1

The sides of the van are from 18mm/¾in blockboard, but they can just as easily be ply, which is even stronger and more weatherproof. The two base pieces, in the same way, are given here as softwood but they can also be ply or blockboard; just check and re-check the dimensions to make sure you have allowed for the possible differences in thickness. For extra strength yet, and a real 'heavy duty' van, the roof sections and front wings can be screwed to the tops of the sides as well as

MATERIALS

Birch plywood		Metric			Imperial		
G Back roof	1	230mm	×193mm	×9	9¹⁄₁₆in×	7⅝in	×⅜in
F Front roof	1	126	×193	×9	5 ×	7⅝	×⅜
H Rear wings	2	140	× 70	×9	5½ ×	2¾	×⅜
Blockboard							
E Sides	2	345	×195	×18	13½ ×	7¾	×¾
Hardwood dowel							
Door hinges	4	40	×	6 dia.	1½ ×	¼ dia.	
Plastic wheels	4	100 dia.			4 dia.		
Steel axles	2	180	×	6.5 dia.	7¼ ×	¼ dia.	
Spring washer hubs	4	6.5 dia. (internal)			4 dia. (internal)		
Screws: Steel csk	8	no. 8 ×	25		no. 8 × 1		

Glasspaper medium, fine
Non toxic acrylic paints or modelling enamels
Non toxic polyurethane varnish
Wood glue and/or epoxy resin glue
Wood filler

TOOLS

Fretsaw or coping saw or electric jigsaw
Tenon saw
Crosscut or panel saw if no jigsaw
Pencil, paper, card, carbon
Steel rule, flexible rule
Try square
Compass
Hand or electric drill
Bits: 6.5mm/¼in, 3mm/⅛in, 32mm/1¼in flat bit, countersink
Hacksaw
Fine cut file
G-cramps
25mm/1in paintbrush
Fine artist's brush
Block or bench plane or Surform shaper plane
Screwdriver

glued; if you decide to do this, use 25mm/1in countersunk bright zinc plated screws, and countersink your clearance holes (5mm/³⁄₁₆in) well so the screws will be concealed and you can fill the recesses. Remember to pilot drill through the holes with a 3mm/⅛in drill before you screw up.

As a final touch, why not paint the owner/driver's name and business on the sides? If you want to do it in 'circular' vintage style like the one in the picture, make up your own template and stencil

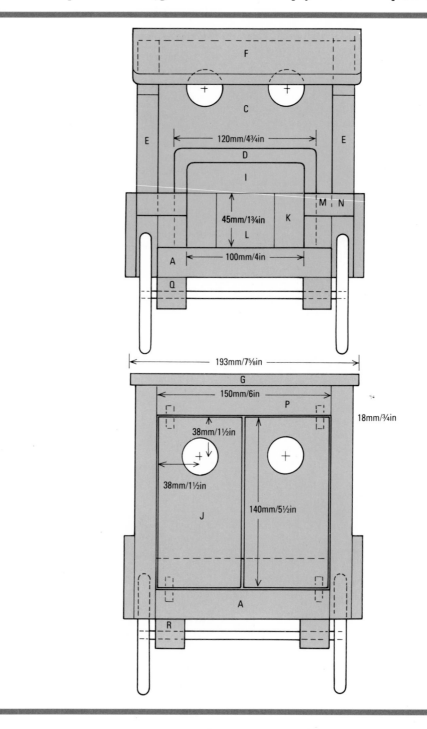

first. Freehand never works well for this sort of job, even for experienced signwriters. Alternatively, you could buy transfers to brighten up the sides of the van; pictures of flowers for a florist, pies and sausages for a butcher, and bread for a baker!

MAIN BODY

1 Measure and cut exactly to length the two base parts A and B. Round over the top front edge of B and glue it to A, lining up the sides and setting the back edge 18mm/¾in forward of the

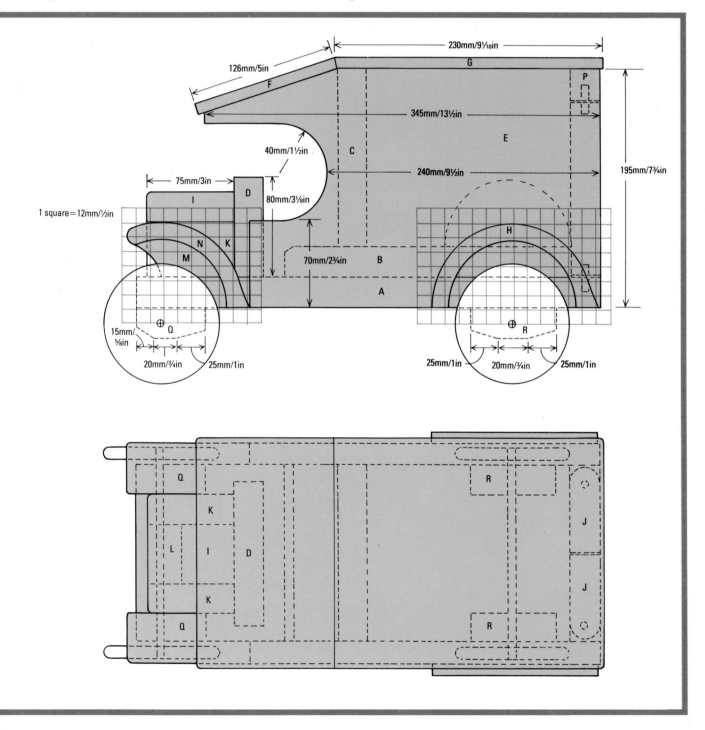

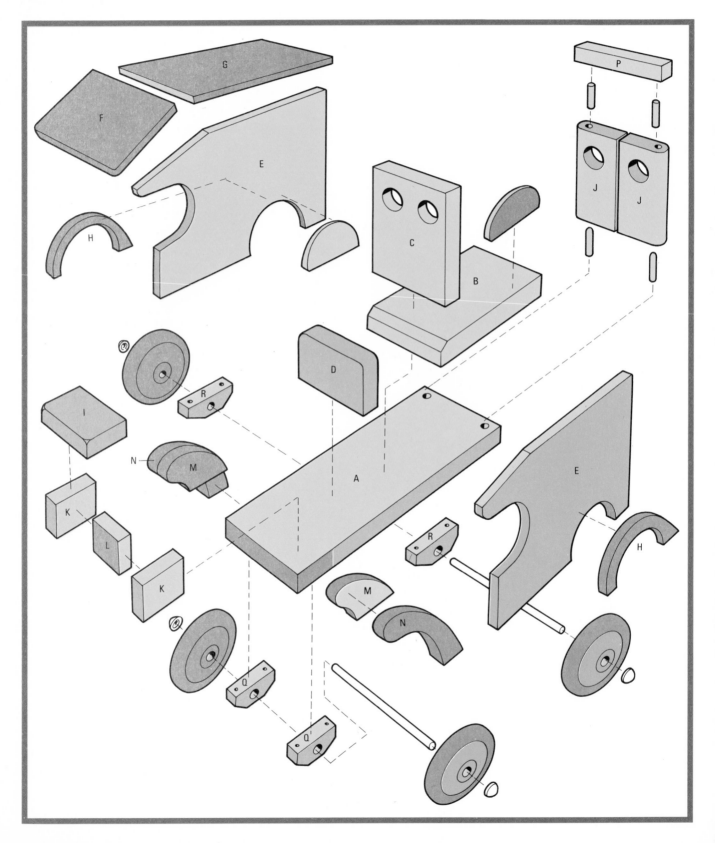

back edge of A. Clamp it or put a weight on the assembly. Measure and cut the two doors J and the bulkhead C and mark and drill the 32mm/1¼in windows. Hold the doors upright in a vice and drill vertical 6.5mm/¼in holes in their outer top edges as shown to a depth of 18mm/¾in.

Round off the outer long edges of the doors with a plane and glasspaper so they will pivot easily.

2 Cut the van sides E to length and width, then draw a 40mm/1½in radius for the arc and transfer the shapes of the cut-outs, and cut them out with the coping saw or jigsaw. Cut the two roof supports P to length and drill the two 6.5mm/¼in holes for the door hinges as shown.

Sand all the parts you have cut so far, paying particular attention to the inside edges of the windows.

3 Glue the sides E and the bulkhead C to the base and to each other, making sure everything lines up dead square. Put blobs of glue on the ends of the roof support P and glue that in between the top back corners of the sides.

Clamp or weight the whole thing together while the glue dries. Cut out the two rear

wings H from the 9mm/⅜in ply, having used your grid to mark out the shapes; sand them and glue them to the sides of the van

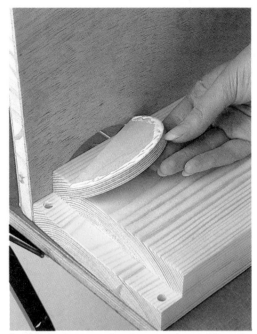

body, lining up the inner edges. Glue the ply offcuts inside the body to blank off the holes.

4 Cut the four blanks for the two front wing components M and N and mark out their shapes from the grid; cut them out with the coping or jigsaw. Glue the inner to outer pieces, remembering to make a left and a right-hand wing. Leave the lower 18mm/¾in of the outer section N protruding from the inner one so it will overlap on to the base when it is in place.

ENGINE

5 Measure, mark and accurately cut to length all the parts of the engine assembly, D,I,K and L. Glue the sides, top and front, I, K and L together, setting the front L back slightly to form a radiator. Round off all the edges when the glue has set, and glue the assembly centrally to the bulkhead D.

FITTING THE DOORS

6 Cut the four 6.5mm/¼in hinge dowels to length and taper them slightly at one end. Drill the pivot holes in the back corners of the body base – right through – and push two dowels, tapered ends first, up through from underneath. Fit the doors on to the dowels and then slide the other two dowels down

HINT
A 'crosscut' or 'panel' saw has a 558–609mm/ 20–24in blade and about 7–10 teeth per 25mm/inch. Remember when cutting panel materials that one side will 'break out'; be sure this is the worst side, and use it in the construction so it will not be seen.

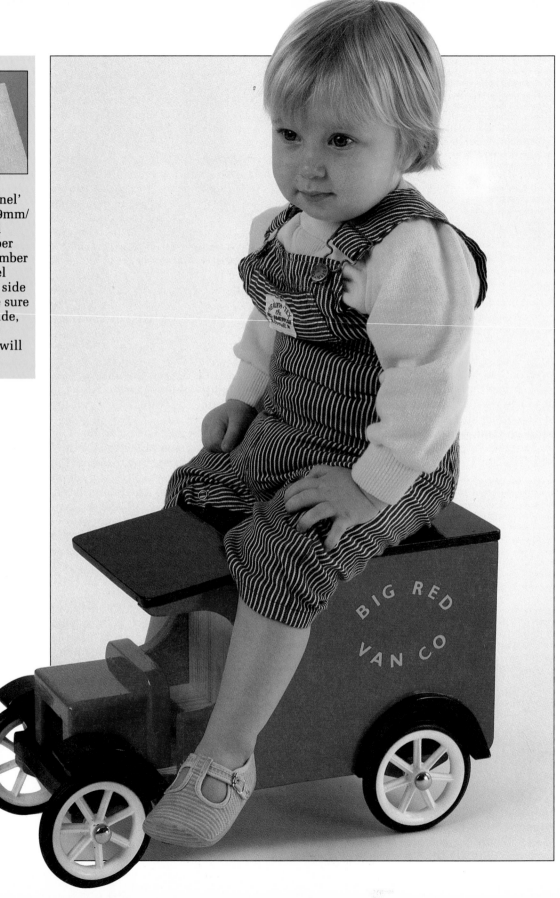

AXLE BEARERS AND WHEELS

8 Cut the four axle bearers to length and shape them with the plane. Drill the holes for the axles and the screws (5mm/³⁄₁₆in) and countersink the latter; square reference lines across the base and glue and screw them in position, the front ones as far forward as possible. The short slope is to the front. Make sure the rear wheels will turn in the wheel arches before you fix the back ones.

9 'Dry assemble' the whole van to make sure everything fits and works. Put the axles in the bearers and work out exactly how long they need to be – don't fit the hubs yet! – and cut them to length with the hacksaw. Take all the unfixed pieces off and sand everything thoroughly, then paint with acrylics and varnish or varnish and modelling enamels in that order. Use at least two coats of varnish, rubbed down gently between each coat with fine glasspaper. If you will use wood glue for the assembly, make sure not to paint the gluing areas; if you use epoxy there is no need.

10 Glue the whole van together, making sure to fit the doors first, and checking when you glue the front wings that there is clearance for the wheels. You can also screw the front wings

through the holes in the roof support P to engage in the holes in the top edges of the doors. If everything is lined up right they should work, but you might need to plane, sand and adjust the doors so they swing properly. When they do, remove the doors and the top dowels and glue the bottom ones in position, trimming them off flush to the underside of the base.

ROOF

7 Mark out and cut the roof sections on the 9mm/³⁄₈in ply, and chamfer across the back edge of the front

section F and the top of the bulkhead C so the two sections fit properly without gaps.

on for strength. Slide the axles in, their wheels on each end, and tap the spring hubs on to complete the vintage van.

USING A GRID

Patterns and designs used for making toys or clothes are rarely printed in books on a life-size scale because they are too big. Thus, plans have to be copied from their small printed size and enlarged acurately so that the pieces will fit together exactly. In this case, the plan will give the size the finished squares need to be (for example 1 square = 25mm/1in).

In this book, only the parts of the projects which involve cutting out irregular shapes have been presented on grids. To get the right proportions, draw out a full size grid (they are usually based on 12mm/½in or 25mm/1in units) on tracing paper, transfer the design to the tracing paper full size, then use carbon paper to transfer the shape from the tracing paper to the wood. When you are using tracing and carbon paper together, tape or pin them both to the wood so they don't move in relation to each other. It often helps to make a scale drawing of your piece of ply, hardboard or timber and

sketch the pieces on to it so you can work out how they can be cut most economically. Never be impatient with drawing – it's easier and cheaper to throw away a piece of paper than a piece of wood you have spent time and money on!

To draw up a design from our plans to any size you want, first look for the largest component, that is, the piece that would cover the largest amount of squares on your grid, from top to bottom, or side to side. If, for example, the piece covers 5½ squares, count to the nearest whole number – that is, 6. Next, decide how big you want the enlarged toy; you may want, for instance, a certain component 420mm/16½in high. In this case, simply divide the number of squares you have counted into 420mm/16½in (420 ÷ 6). This equals 70, so all you do is draw up a grid with squares of 70mm/2¾in. Copy the design on to this so that the lines fall on the grid lines in the same way as the original.

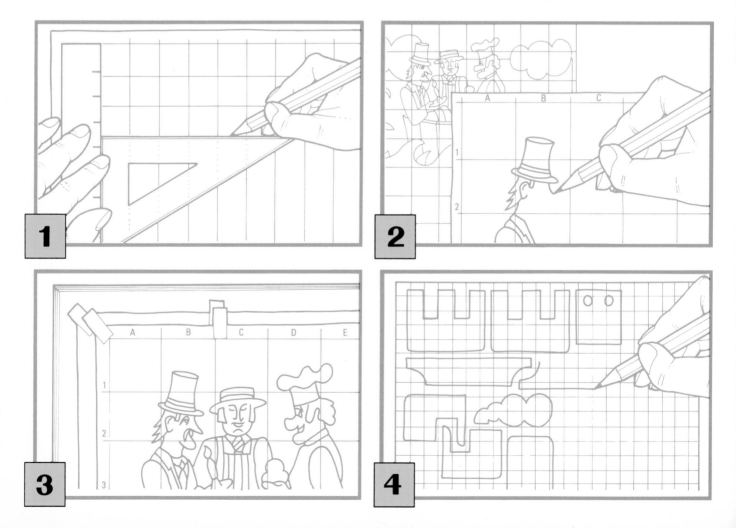

INDEX

INDEX

ACKNOWLEDGEMENTS

The publishers would like to extend special thanks to the following for their help in the production of this book:

Models

Charlotte Burke	Tommy Fraser
Jeff Burke	Jay Patel
Cordelia Canning	Preya Patel
Rebecca Dewing	Sima Patel
Victoria Dewing	Gabriel Pitcher

Props
Hamleys, Regent Street, London
Playmobiles (UK) Ltd
The Reject Shop, Tottenham Court Road, London

Picture
Supermarine SEB (p20) Austin J Brown aviation picture library

Popular Science Books offers a wood identification kit that includes 30 samples of cabinet woods. For details on ordering, please write: Popular Science Books, P.O. Box 2033, Latham, N.Y. 12111.

Rub a dub dub
Three men in a tub
The butcher, the baker
And the candlestickmaker